THE SPANISH COOKBOOK

BARBARA NORMAN

THE
SPANISH
COOKBOOK

ATHENEUM   NEW YORK

1966

PARA MARÍA Y PEPITO

FOREWORD

THE recipes in this book are all authentic Spanish recipes, not adapted ones. Rather than adapt, which is in some sense to falsify, I have omitted dishes requiring hours of work or unobtainable ingredients: there are so many simple and excellent Spanish recipes that can be made in the traditional manner with little effort. Many of them are convenient one-dish meals; many can be made in thirty minutes or less.

The yields of a recipe are given in terms of the number of average servings rather than the number of people served. Second or larger-than-average servings should be calculated according to the number of courses, the richness of the dish, and the probable appetites of the guests.

In the collection of these recipes and the material for the text, I have been given extremely generous assistance by many Spanish chefs, restaurant owners, official organizations, and private individuals. It would be impossible to list all the people who have contributed in some way to the making of this book, but I wish in particular to express my gratitude to Señor and Señora José Solé of Restaurante

Pi, Vendrell (Tarragona), who first introduced me to Spanish cooking at its best; to Señora Elvira Blanco de Nombela, cookbook author and journalist, who gave recipes and advice so liberally; to Señor Andrés Soler Monsalve, representative of Bodegas Bilbaínas, who tirelessly tracked down information I sought on food and wine; to Señor José Marlés, whose invaluable hints contributed so much; to Señor Candido Tojal Varela, who is responsible for much of the information on Basque cooking techniques; to the gastronomic authority and journalist Señor Juan Cabané; and to Mr. Joseph Ravotto, Press Attaché of the United States Embassy in Madrid; the Ministerio de Información y Turismo; the Sindicato Nacional de Hostelería y Similares; the Sindicato Nacional de la Vid; the Sindicato Nacional del Olivo; the Cooperativa Nacional del Arroz; and the Consejo Regulador de la Denominación de Origen Jerez-Xérès-Sherry.

CONTENTS

CONTENTS

THE SPANISH COOKBOOK

CHAPTER I

WHAT IS SPANISH COOKING?

SPANISH food, like that of all countries, varies greatly from region to region while preserving a national character as if it were stamped *Made in Spain*. Almost everyone who has eaten any Spanish food is familiar with paella. But what makes that and other dishes Spanish? In general, Spanish cooking is uncomplicated, depending for its savor on freshness of the ingredients, care in the timing, and restraint in the seasoning. (Spanish food, by the way, should not be confused with the spicy cuisine of Mexico, with which it has almost nothing in common.)

In Spain, food is often boiled or broiled, then made tasty with a simple sauce. The juice of the meat or fish forms the base of the sauce, and flavoring is added only to heighten its natural qualities. Flavoring may be a matter of eight or nine crushed almonds, a sprig of thyme, or the tip of a bay leaf. No complicated procedures, no unobtainable, exotic ingredients are necessary. Garlic is sometimes used heavily, but you can modify the amount to suit your taste just as you salt and pepper to taste. Tomatoes and onions are the foundation of countless sauces, and, as in almost all Mediterranean countries, olive oil replaces butter in most recipes. Peppers and paprika are constantly used; parsley is employed in quantities that make it a distinct condiment, not just a green decoration, and the delicious cured ham available everywhere in Spain flavors dishes from soup and eggs to shellfish and chicken.

The Spanish eat late; very late. To fill in the long stretches between meals, there are a number of snacks, heavy or light according to the size of the other meals. The day begins with the *desayuno* (*day-sah-you'noh*), or breakfast, normally no more than a cup of coffee or chocolate, perhaps with bread and jam or a sweet roll. The second meal, the *almuerzo* (*al-mwer'tho*), taken in midmorning, is a more serious affair: an omelet accompanied by bread and wine; an open sandwich of bread smeared with a ripe tomato, sprinkled with olive oil, and covered with cured ham or sausage; or even a hot meal of beans and grilled sausage, fish, lamb chops, or any other dish that might appear on a dinner menu.

The main meal of the day, the *comida* (*co-mee'dah*), is eaten at two or three in the afternoon and usually starts with a salad, followed by a fish course, a meat course, and fruit or some other light dessert. Toward six o'clock, it is time for the *merienda* (*meh-ree-en'dah*). Often a very light snack—a bit of bread with honey or coffee and cookies—if there are guests, it will be an elaborate meal with cold omelets, ham, sausages, fish croquettes, cold fish,

4

cold meats, and a variety of salads. The last meal, or *cena* (*thay'nah*), is normally about ten o'clock, but may be any time between eight-thirty and midnight. At home, this is a light supper, but again, if there is company, a celebration, or an outing to a restaurant, it will be a full-course dinner.

As you can see, the variation in the hours and kinds of meals is enormous. In consequence, the average Spanish restaurant is open most of the time from early morning to midnight, ready to serve almost anything at almost any instant from baby octopus and steak at eight in the morning to a five-course banquet at midnight. One of the greatest shocks Spaniards suffer when traveling abroad for the first time is that they can no longer get anything they want to eat any time they want it: why, a restaurant may close its doors to them from two in the afternoon until six or eight at night, and even then only open for an hour or so!

The culinary level varies widely throughout Spain, from the rudimentary cooking of the hot plains of central Andalusia or the barren steppes of Castile to the highly developed arts of the two areas that produce the greatest food: the Basque country and Catalonia, the northwest and northeast corners of Spain. The lean Spaniards of the south will celebrate a marriage or a christening with a feast appropriate to the occasion, but are otherwise content to live on olives, wine, bread, tomatoes, and whatever else falls to hand.

CATALONIA

The Catalan cuisine is as distinct from that of the rest of Spain as are the language and customs of Catalonia, an area of roughly 12,500 square miles forming a broad strip along the Mediterranean coast from the French-Spanish border to Valencia. The Catalans are a broad-faced, smiling race, proud of their ancient heritage (Catalonia was once an independent kingdom), hearty eaters, and decidedly on the heavy side. The visitor to Catalonia soon discovers that it is not for nothing that talk in that area almost always turns to ways of growing, catching, and eating food.

Of course, some of the dainties appreciated locally may not appeal to the non-native: baby octopus in a sauce of garlic and pounded almonds, tripe in tomato sauce, or fried chicken blood with liver, to name a few. But there are numerous tempting items, many of which are easy to reproduce in an American kitchen.

One of the delights of eating in this region is the succession of new foods following the changes of season: almost every month heralds a new delicacy. At about the time the first strawberries appear in northern Europe, Catalonians near the sea are feasting on stews of *tallinas* (*tal-yee'nas*), pearly-shelled clams an inch long, plentiful on the beaches in May. Professional fishermen drag for them with rakes that take two men to pull, but amateurs can quickly gather enough for supper along the water's edge using a small garden rake with a net attached. The cooking of *tallinas* is as simple as the eating, and the recipe (p. 118) can be used for mussels or any kind of clams available in your area.

When the supply of *tallinas* grows short, the melon season opens, and everyone gorges on melons twice a day. Because each melon has its own personality, its own flavor and consistency, one never tires of them. If, however, there are too many on hand, they can be stored away to be eaten

6

as late as Christmas or, in very dry years, Easter. In September, the market is flooded with baby fish, usually served fried lightly in olive oil and eaten whole, sometimes as a main dish, often as an appetizer with a glass of sherry before dinner. The bones, head, and tail are as soft as the inside of a fried potato.

The opening of the hunting season on October 1 brings a new gamut of dishes to the table and new topics to the conversation. Partridge hunters are split into two fiercely opposed groups according to the method of hunting they prefer, and the arguments over which is the least "criminal" and most effective are long and heated. In one method, the hunter carries to the field a caged partridge (which he has kept all year for this purpose). The singing of the caged bird attracts a partridge of the opposite sex, who is downed by the hunter at the moment the bird is blissfully expecting to meet its mate. Hunters of the second group, who tramp cross-country with a dog to flush the bird, argue that the first method is treacherous, unsporting, and immoral. One partisan of the caged-bird method described it as a delightful way to pass the afternoon: stretched out comfortably in the grass, listening to bird calls—the kind of afternoon that leaves a man with energy and good humor, whether he catches anything or not. On the other hand, the argument continues, the traditional hunter who chases an elusive prey for mile after mile is apt to return home exhausted and grouchy, with neither enough good humor to joke with his friends nor enough energy to take his wife to the movies.

A traditional Catalan way of serving partridge is pan roasted and accompanied by cabbage croquettes (p. 150), delicious morsels which would go equally well with goose or roast pork on a fall Sunday. Partridge and pheasants are

7

the birds most hunted, but almost any bird is likely to be shot and put in the casserole. One of the more unusual quarries is the owl. The way to catch this bird, I have been told, is to paint a rock white, place a white board coated with glue on the rock after dark, and wait for the owl to become stuck in the glue. The enthusiasts claim owl meat is very rich and worth the trouble.

Wild hare weighing as much as 10 pounds are occasionally shot during the hunting season in Catalonia. A tempting way of cooking your hare in the fields if you do not want to wait till you reach home to eat it, is to spear it in spreadeagle position with sticks of rosemary bush, brace it over a wood fire on four stones, and roast it while basting with mustard and garlic sauce. The full recipe is on page 224, and others for preparing rabbit or hare in the calm of the kitchen on pages 148–149.

In October and November, particularly after a rainfall, the hills and forests are scoured by another brand of hunter: the mushroom hunter. There are said to be at least four hunters for every mushroom in Catalonia. This makes mushroom hunting a fiercely competitive sport. The most successful are those who know exactly where the mushrooms are likely to appear year after year, a jealously guarded secret. Of the dozen edible varieties, the most highly prized is the *rovellon,* which, like the *cêpe* of southern France, has a rich, meaty flavor. To show its flavor to the greatest advantage, the *rovellon* is usually simply grilled and served with a little olive oil, chopped garlic, and parsley. The more ordinary mushrooms are fried with garlic and parsley or put in a sauce you will find on page 177. In most of Spain, mushrooms are available only in the fall because they are not grown commercially (at least not on a wide scale). Those gathered in the fall are put in brine and preserved for later use in an extremely simple way, recommended to anyone who has access to wild mushrooms (p. 186).

In December, artichokes are ripe but still small enough to be eaten whole. They are prepared in many ways: stuffed, fried, grilled, and in omelets (see pp. 170–172), or are used in sauces. The weather is chilly now, especially when the sun goes down, and that is the hour at which villagers go to the local olive press carrying with them bread in thick slices for *la rosta*. The owner or operator of the press keeps wine and garlic on hand to complete the menu and receives those who come as guests. The purpose of the custom is to give all buyers or users a chance to test the quality of the new olive oil. It is warm inside the room where the oil is trickling between layers of straw mats and being piped from one refining machine to another until it pours out, hot and clear gold, into tile vats about four times the size of a bathtub. The guests toast their slices of bread on long forks over the coals of the stove, rub the bread with garlic if they like, then plunge it into the hot, virgin oil of the first pressing. The result is *la rosta*—messy to eat, but remarkably good. The new oil has a special taste akin to that of freshly roasted nuts, and has little in common with the flavor of olive oil even one month old. One *rosta* makes you want another, and after two, you don't need any supper.

In February, the broad beans ripen. Because the season of young beans is short, they are served very often at this time of year. One of the favorite methods of fixing them —smothered, with sausage—makes a sumptuous one-dish meal (p. 176). Curly endive salad is now at its best, and the Catalonians combat the cold by eating Xató (*cha-toh'*), a peppery salad of curly endive served with an assortment of meats, sausages, and omelets (p. 55).

In the early spring, the asparagus hunter roams the fields. The wild green stalks found growing under the carob trees and along dry riverbeds are a much-sought-after delicacy, although the hunting of them on sunny spring days when the field flowers are in full bloom is probably a large part of the pleasure. The spring onions ripen at the same time, and restaurants specializing in this dish provide paper bibs to protect their clients while they strip the charred skins from the charcoal grilled onions and dip them in peppery sauce (p. 193). And soon the *tallinas* become plentiful again, and a year of eating will have made a full circle.

THE BASQUE PROVINCES

The rival region of good eating in Spain is the Basque country, that part of Spain in the upper northwest corner inhabited by a race of still mysterious origin whose native language, Basque, bears no relation to Spanish. Although the Basque area spills over into southwestern France, aside from a common language and origin Spanish Basques and French Basques resemble each other little. The Basque men in Spain are big-boned, broad-shouldered, stout eaters, hearty drinkers, and lusty singers. It is the men who have made and kept Basque cooking famous, and it is not unusual for the husband to return to his house in the evening to prepare his own fish in his own way.

Aside from singing, dancing, and drinking, one of the main social activities of the Spanish Basque is cooking and eating. This pastime has given rise to the founding of many gastronomic societies, all exclusively male. Here the men cook and eat enormous banquets, each man preparing or collaborating on some dish he does particularly well. San Sebastián, a pretty port town near the French border, is the originator and center of these gastronomic societies. The first was founded in 1870. There are now over thirty in San Sebastián, two in Bilbao, and a few in other Basque towns, particularly throughout the province of Guipuzcoa, all modeled after those of San Sebastián. The societies maintain excellent choirs and are dedicated to the upholding of culinary traditions and the support of charity. Some well-known Basque dishes have been created in the societies, and others owe their fame and popularity to them.

The locale of an eating society is equipped with a dining room furnished with long wooden tables seating twelve to twenty, a kitchen with numerous burners and ovens, larders, a wine cellar, a cold-storage room, plates, glasses, linens—all the apparatus of a restaurant. Each member has a key, enters when he pleases, and stays as long as he likes. On weekdays there are usually a few dozen members having appetizers and wine between 7 and 10 P.M., and two or three cooking a meal which will be eaten by anyone who stays late and grows hungry. On Saturday evenings, the societies are full.

The organization is extremely informal. If a man happens to be given a nice sea bream as a present, he may invite a few friends and set off for his society with a market basket containing what he needs to cook his fish. The more ordinary staples, as well as coffee, liqueurs, and wine, are kept in stock, each item being the charge of some member. Wine and cider are bought in barrels and bottled on the premises. Each member makes out his own bill for wine, staples, the use of the stove and linens, and leaves the money in a kitty. It is the pride of San Sebastián that when the count is made at the end of the year, there is always money left over.

The size of the society varies with the size of the locale. Some have forty to sixty members; three of the most active have many more—from one hundred to two hundred. The membership is the most democratic imaginable, including, in the same society, fishermen and bank presidents, all of whom sit side by side on the benches lining the long tables. The dues are a quarter a month. The only exclusion is that of women, who are traditionally allowed to enter the sanctuary on the eve of Assumption Day (August 15) and Saint Sebastian's Day (January 20). Otherwise, the only woman is the one in charge of cleaning up afterward.

The staggering capacity of the Basques for food and wine never ceases to astound the non-Basque. Two Basques can happily consume one entire roast kid without any difficulty, but they are as demanding of quality as of quantity. According to *La Cocina de Nicolasa,** the book of recipes from the famous restaurant Casa Nicolasa in San Sebastián, there is no mention in early chronicles of an outstanding cuisine in the Basque country, and it probably did not come into being until economic progress transformed the north of Spain in the nineteenth century. The gastronomic importance of San Sebastián developed only after the town became the capital of the province of Guipuzcoa. This is not to say that the foundations of some dishes may not be hundreds of years old: it is the refinement that is recent.

The Basques are extremely particular about the seasons and origin of foods. In April and May, they eat tiny, dark,

* Nicolasa Pradera. Madrid: Editorial Mayfe, 1961.

tasty mushrooms available only then. In April, May, and June, they eat a vegetable dish made with the most tender and diminutive spring vegetables, grown in specific sites (Menestra de Legumbres, p. 181). Every Basque knows the season each fish is at its best and from what part of the coast it should come to be most succulent. A dish called Kokotxas (pronounced *co-co'chas*) is an illustration of the subtlety of the Basque cuisine. The *kokotxa* is the part of hake cut from the head just under the chin and following the line of the chin. It is considered the most delicate part of the fish and spoils first, which is one reason for its removal before the fish is shipped to the interior. The *kokotxas* are sold in the market by the pound, piled high in baskets. They are usually cooked with a little garlic, parsley, and green peas. Being very gelatinous, they are particularly suitable for simmering in the Basque manner.

Pil-pil is a Basque expression meaning "simmered," and one of the fundamentals of Basque cooking is typified in the recipe for Bacalao Pil-pil (p. 126). The dish is little more than strips of the most gelatinous parts of cod cooked very slowly in an earthenware casserole in olive oil. While it cooks, the casserole is jiggled and swirled from time to time (never stirred) until the sauce thickens by the blending of the fish juices with the olive oil. The same principle of cooking in an earthenware casserole over a slow fire and moving the casserole occasionally until the juice of the fish or the starch of the potatoes forms a sauce applies to innumerable Basque dishes. The secret of the blending lies in the temperature of the olive oil, which must be just simmering when the fish or potatoes are added. The timing for some of the recipes seems long—twenty minutes for a slice of hake, for

13

example—but in this method of cooking, all the time is put to good use.

Another characteristic of Basque sauces is restraint in seasoning. The most common sauces are either red or green: red with peppers and tomatoes; green with parsley and, perhaps, peas and asparagus tips. Because the lush, grassy hills of the Basque country allow the grazing of cattle, in Basque kitchens you find cream, so heavily used just the other side of the Pyrenees and so seldom mentioned in Spanish recipes except for desserts.

GALICIA

While there is an abundance of fish in the Basque country (and the Basque cuisine reaches its height of perfection in the cooking of fish), Galicia, the area just north of Portugal, is even more famous for the quality and variety of its seafood, and particularly shellfish. There are the little rock barnacles known as *percebes,* which look like miniature elephants' feet and are eaten raw. There is a kind of scallop, the *vieira,* whose shells pilgrims traditionally carried to Santiago de Compostela. There is an enormous variety of clams of all sizes and shapes, small crabs of diverse sizes and colors, and the famous *centolla* (or *shangurro*), a giant crab weighing 5 pounds or more.

Galicia is green, rainy, extremely rich agriculturally, and produces foods of a particular savor: Galicians sing praises of their succulent tomatoes, pungent onions, rich potatoes (of which they eat quantities), and their fruits, which, except for grapes, are excellent. Because the natu-

ral products are so good, Galician cooking is uncomplicated—so much so, that Galicia might be referred to in
culinary terms as the country of boiling. "Boiling" con-
jures up visions of overcooked, watery, and tasteless
spinach, but that is totally unrelated to the Galician
boiling. There, boiling is an art just as frying is in
southern Spain: because the cooking is done to perfection
and the product is the best and the freshest, nothing more
could be wanted.

Galicians know how to compose a dish too, however.
Among the favorite foods is the Empanada Gallega, a
bread-shaped, covered pie that can have any number of
fillings, all of which begin with the frying of a quantity of
onions: cod, red peppers, and onions; fried fish with
onions; or a variety of meats with onions (see pp.
109–110). The empanada is a hearty one-dish meal eaten
hot or cold, and a favorite for eating in the fields,
particularly on chilly days. The delightful so-called
"green" wine of the Ribeiro completes the menu hand-
somely.

Another favorite is Lacón con Grelos (cured foreham
with turnip greens), which, because of the particular and
characteristic flavor of the Galician-cured forehams and
the contrasting bitterness of the local turnip greens,
cannot be duplicated elsewhere. The dish which is Galician par excellence, however, is the Galician meat and
vegetable soup, Caldo Gallego, with its strong flavor of
aged ham (p. 75). The desserts, generally made on the
basis of traditional monastery recipes, are usually composed of pounded almonds and egg yolks, and are deli-
ciously rich. Tarta de Santiago (p. 211) is a good
example.

The Caldo Gallego has an unusual role in a hearty meal. Although normally served, like any other soup, at the beginning of the meal, at a banquet it is drunk after the main course. Another Galician tradition is the *té quemada,* which follows dessert. A fairly deep earthenware bowl is put in the middle of the table with liqueur from the Ribeiro, the main wine-producing area of Galicia. Sugar lumps and a little lemon rind are added; the liquid is lighted and stirred while it burns, then a bit of coffee is poured in, and the *té quemada* is drunk in coffee cups dipped directly in the bowl.

THE ASTURIAS

Lying between the Basque country and Galicia are the Asturias, a land far apart in customs and cooking from either of the two. This is the land of cider, not wine, a cider with a pleasantly odd sour taste which is an excellent accompaniment to the hearty stew called Fabada, named after a special, large white bean in the shape of a half moon known as the *fabe* and grown only in certain regions of the Asturias. The Fabada, a stew of these white beans slowly simmered with *lacón,* hung beef, Asturian sausages, and *chorizo* cured in wood-smoke, has acquired worldwide fame and is even exported in cans to America. Unfortunately, its recipe cannot be duplicated without the native products, only imitated. To eat it, other than canned, you must go to the Asturias or to a Madrid restaurant that imports the necessary ingredients, such as the Casa Mingo, whose owner claims his Fabada excels those made in the Asturias because of the superior quality of Madrid water. The Asturias also offer fish soups and fish stews, a variety of game, and make rather extensive use of corn—in corn pudding and corn bread, for example. As is to be expected in a land of cider, there are very good apples. The cider is used in cooking, as wine is in other areas.

The Asturians have been partial to cider for twenty centuries: the Greek geographer Strabo wrote of Asturian cider nearly 2,000 years ago. Today there are 2,700 factories in the Asturias turning out over 7,000,000 gallons of natural cider annually, of which 6,000,000 are consumed by the Asturians themselves. Effervescent cider is an important export, particularly appreciated in Cuba, Argentina, and Puerto Rico. According to the house of Sidras Mingo, the exportation of effervescent cider constituted the most reliable and important source of foreign currency for the Spanish government prior to the recent influx of tourists.

The way of drinking cider is a ritual peculiar to the Asturians. The bottle is held high overhead in one hand and the cider is poured into a glass in the upturned palm of the other hand, held as close to the ground as possible. An expert can pour it without looking. The liquid is supposed to fall without much force against the side of the tilted glass and to descend slowly into the bottom. This causes the formation of a natural carbonic gas, which gives the drink a most agreeable flavor. In fact, once they have drunk the foam, the Asturians toss out any remaining liquid, usually directly on the floor. In Asturian reunions it used to be customary to use only one glass. Each drank from it in turn, emptying the remains in such a manner as to rinse the part of the glass touched by his lips.

17

NAVARRE AND ARAGON

Between the Basque country and Catalonia, Navarre and Aragon meet across the north of Spain. Both are fond of fixing meats and fowl a la Chilindrón (p. 166)— stewed with ground pepper, red peppers, and tomatoes, or Cochifrito (p. 167)—browned with garlic, lemon juice, paprika, and ground pepper. There is no coastline here, but the rivers provide trout, which may be served in red wine seasoned with mint and rosemary or stuffed with cured ham (p. 140).

MADRID & OLD AND NEW CASTILE

The high central plateaus of Spain are the land of roasting: suckling pig and baby lamb roasted in wood-burning ovens are to be found in the area of the ancient kingdoms of León and Castile. This is a country of shepherds, who have developed a strong-flavored, hearty, and unsophisticated cuisine. Among the popular dishes, as always, we find a vegetable-meat soup, distinguished by the use of *chorizo* sausage and chick-peas. There are Callos a la Madrileña, or tripe cooked somewhat like tripe à la mode de Caen of France, and there are a number of delectable pastry specialties.

While Madrid has given some dishes its name, there is no true Madrid cuisine. On the other hand, being the geographical center of Spain, the juncture of all railways, and the capital, Madrid gives any visitor the opportunity to eat the best of everything in the country prepared in the

18

manner of each region. Here the delicate seafood of the coasts of Galicia is rushed in, pearly fresh, to the Galician restaurants, along with the rarely exported, heady Galician wines; the slow-cooking sauces of the Basques are produced with fish fresh from the Basque coast; the hearty Fabada of the Asturias is stewed with all the specially cured ingredients smoked and aged in their native province; the spectacular Catalan chicken and lobster a la Costa Brava is served in its bright red sauce; and the fish soups are those you might eat on the coast near Cádiz, preceded by a glass of amber sherry which seems to embody all the sun and sea of Jerez de la Frontera. Every regional delicacy from elsewhere in Spain is concentrated in Madrid. However, if you are in Madrid and insist on eating something distinctly Madrileño, have chocolate for breakfast and dip in it those fried batter sticks with the ridged sides known as *churros*.

ANDALUSIA

Going south from Madrid, we come to the vast area of Andalusia, the land of gazpacho and—as might be expected in the province producing most of the olive oil of the world's chief olive-producing country—the land of supremely expert frying. The Andalusians fry fish better than anyone in the world. For some reason, they all put the right amount of flour on the fish to keep it intact, they all have the exact amount of oil at the precise heat necessary to seize and crispen the outside of the fish, and they all know the moment the inside is cooked but still moist. All it takes is fresh fish, an unsparing use of good olive oil, and a little critical practice.

One of the most delicious possible lunches, if you live where baby fish can be bought fresh, is a green salad followed by the fish, cleaned (with little opening), headless, passed lightly in salted flour, fried in very hot olive oil at least ¼ inch deep until golden brown, and served instantly. The Andalusians always throw the fish into the hot oil in threes or fours, pinched together at the tail and spread out in a fan shape. If the fish are tiny, you eat them bones and all. If not, the only reasonable way to consume them is to pick the small fish up in your fingers and eat the meat off the bone like corn on the cob.

Frying has the advantage of quick preparation, which may also contribute to the popularity of gazpacho throughout this region of long hot summers. Gazpacho has an ancient history, being descended from the Alboronía of the Andalusian Moors. It is made and used in so many ways that it defies classification. Outside Spain (or outside Andalusia, for that matter), it is usually classified as a soup. That, I have been told by a native of Seville, is almost an insult. For the Andalusian peasants and laborers, gazpacho is the entire midday meal and all that is eaten between early morning and sunset on hot summer days. At the tables of the rich, it is served in various ways: as a first course, as a liquid accompanying the main part of the meal, as a salad, and even as a midday dessert in place of fruit. (Pastries and heavy desserts are seldom served at noon in the Andalusian heat.)

In its humblest form, gazpacho may contain nothing more than garlic, bread, olive oil, wine vinegar, water, and salt; in its more bourgeois version, onion, cucumbers, green peppers, and tomatoes or even almonds and egg yolks may be added. The most startling is probably the gazpacho of Málaga, Ajo Blanco con Uvas, which, trans-

lated literally, means "white garlic with grapes." White
garlic is a term for the basic or humble gazpacho without
the addition of egg yolks or chopped vegetables; the
grapes are peeled white grapes which float on top. The
Gazpacho Manchego of Don Quixote's land, La Mancha,
is so unlike the others that one wonders at its title: it is a
thick, unleavened bread porridge mixed with cooked game
meats. Recipes for a variety of regional gazpachos are
given on pages 60–63.

The coast from Málaga to the Portuguese border is
famous for the variety and delicacy of its fish, some of
which are found nowhere else. There is a shellfish akin to
an oyster, the *ostion,* which is only good cooked—fried or
baked; there are the *chanquetes,* or small anchovy, which
are a specialty of Málaga; there are tiny shrimp served in
fritters, unique species of clams, and, as in all coastal areas
of Spain, there are a number of local ways of preparing
fish soups and stews. The province in which sherry is made
is naturally the home of many dishes made with sherry:
kidneys, oxtails, chicken, etc., and Seville is the originator
of the well-known Huevos a la Flamenca (p. 90).

THE LEVANTE

The area of rice and paella begins in Murcia, east of
Andalusia and south of Catalonia. Rice dominates the
menu all through the Levante, as this strip along the southeastern Mediterranean coast is known. Aside from what
most of us have encountered under the name of Paella
Valenciana (which, as explained in the section on rices,
has little to do with the Valencian concept of paella), the
variety of rice dishes is unending. Anything can go into

the paella from tiny birds to lobsters, from chick-peas to artichokes, from bacon to roast veal. Invented out of necessity, the paella has become a delicacy known throughout the world.

The Levantine coast is also the home of an extraordinary variety of pastries—extraordinary even for Spain, which abounds in such specialties. One of the specialties is the *turrón,* half candybar, half cake, eaten as a dessert at Christmas time throughout Catalonia and the province of Valencia. Extremely rich, of diverse contents (marchpane, nougat, caramelized cream cake, chocolate, or honey and hazelnuts), it is in such demand that in one town alone there are forty factories making *turrón.* Enterprising Alicantinos have even founded a factory in New York where workers who are also from Alicante are busy turning out *turrón.*

IS THERE A NATIONAL SPANISH CUISINE?

Many regional cuisines have been mentioned, but no national Spanish dishes. The question: Is there a national Spanish cuisine? has been raised by many Spanish chefs and other authorities, most of whom agree there is none. Instead, there is what is so fast disappearing from the rest of the world—distinct regional cooking. It is true that you find paella in some form all over Spain, flan (a caramel custard) and spongecake in all restaurants, a kind of pot-au-feu and a garlic soup in every farmhouse from Córdoba to Bilbao to Barcelona, but each area has its own way of preparing these dishes and often looks with distaste upon the way it is made in the neighboring province. The

Valencians find the mixture of fish and meat in the Barcelona paella barbaric; the Catalans are appalled by the peppery food of the Estremadurans; the Madrileños consider Málaga's famous gazpacho merely a culinary curiosity; the Andalusians dislike the Catalan taste for sweets with meats, and so on, ad infinitum. The argument might be summed up by calling Spanish cooking a regional cuisine with national characteristics.

Spanish cooking has a common history. Like so many things, it started with the Romans, whose occupying troops brought the two staples that are the basic elements of the Spanish cuisine: olive oil and garlic. The pounded almonds so often used in Spanish sauces were common to the Romans too. Next the Moors, who occupied Spain for eight centuries, came with their saffron, cumin seed, black pepper, nutmeg, peppermint, lemons, and oranges. All these are still in frequent use as flavorings, along with cinnamon, which came somewhat later when spices were brought directly from the Far East. Spices were highly prized—and highly priced—in the sixteenth and seventeenth centuries. Incredible quantities of the dearly sought condiments were consumed at court and in aristocratic houses. A single sauce of that time contained, for example, salt, pepper, nutmeg, bay leaf, cloves, garlic, cinnamon, benjamin, juniper berries, and thyme, in addition to butter, grape juice, white wine, vinegar, and chicken stock. Spain, importing from her colonies, was in a favorable position to indulge in these luxuries, but she was not alone: France, too, was pouring spices into foods, and except that France was more restrained in the use of cinnamon and sugar, the culinary excesses of the two countries were on a par.

The revolution in Spanish cooking came with the

introduction of the tomato, the pepper, and the potato from America. Although known from the time of the discovery of America, they only came into use in Spain in the eighteenth century, and even more time passed before they became basic elements in Spanish cooking. These three vegetables are now so much a part of Spanish cooking that it is hard to remember, or to believe, that they were incorporated in the national cuisine so recently. There is hardly a dish that does not call for tomato, peppers, or one of the pepper derivatives, paprika or cayenne. As for potatoes, there are half a hundred ways of preparing them recognized as authentic regional dishes, not to speak of the infinite number of meat and fish recipes in which potatoes are an integral part.

The origins of the authentic regional dishes that constitute the Spanish cuisine are humble. They always go back to the fisherman and the peasant, making use of the products at hand and often putting them all in one pot. The humbleness of their origin does not mean they are not worthy of respect. Many are the Spanish dishes happily adopted by the French and generally thought of as part of the classic French cuisine.

A number of these dishes were introduced to France by the Spanish wives of three French sovereigns. Anne of Austria, Infanta of Spain and wife of Louis XIII, introduced stuffed Spanish pastries known as empanadillas, eels "Royal Style," and Sauce Espagnole, among others. Another Spanish Infanta, Maria Theresa, married Louis XIV, and, abhorring all French dishes, brought with her a Spanish cook named La Molina who contributed to the French repertory. In addition, all the recipes entitled *"à l'Eugénie"* or *"à l'impératrice"* (Riz à l'Impératrice, for example) trace their Spanish origin through Eugenia de

Montijo, wife of Napoleon III.

Other Spanish recipes found their way to France through the writer Alexandre Dumas. The Duc de Richelieu is credited with importing to France a sauce called *"mahonesa"* (presumably mayonnaise) from Mahon in the Balearic Islands. When Napoleon I's troops sacked the library of the Monastery of Alcántara on the way to Portugal in 1807, the friars' recipe book was saved from destruction and eventually came into the hands of the wife of General Junot, whose chef, the famous Carême, introduced a number of the friars' dishes to France. The great French chef Escoffier refers to the recipe for Pheasant à la Mode d'Alcántara as the only benefit gained from Napoleon's Portuguese campaign.

OLIVE OIL AND OTHER BASIC ELEMENTS

The basic elements of Spanish cooking, those contributing to its national character, have been mentioned briefly throughout this chapter. Let us now examine them in more detail. First among them is olive oil. It is natural that the olive should be used liberally in Spain. Spain not only leads all countries in olive-oil production, it is far ahead of Italy, which holds second place. Although butter is used occasionally in the north of Spain and lard in certain dishes anywhere, olive oil is the basic cooking and pastry fat.

Devotees of olive oil can assemble many arguments in its favor. There is the historical importance of olives: the olive as the first tree mentioned in Genesis, the olive as the symbol of peace, the olive as a crown for Roman victors, and so on. From the medical point of view, it is argued that olive oil is the most easily digested fat and contains no cholesterol. The Spanish national olive trade association (Sindicato Nacional del Olivo) claims the use of olive oil is economical because it contains 100 percent usable fat, whereas lard has only 76 percent and butter 85 percent. Be that as it may, the advantages of frying with olive oil over frying with butter are obvious to anyone who has done both: the butter, if not clarified or mixed with some oil, burns almost at once, while the olive oil remains intact. Furthermore, the oil's higher burning temperature permits heating it until it will seize and crispen the outside of fish or meat without permeating the flesh. Unlike butter, olive oil can be reused several times if strained.

Spain exports so much of its finest oil that Spaniards in some areas have to put up with an inferior grade. To purify the flavor of poorly refined oil, many Spanish recipes, particularly those for pastries, call for the use of olive oil *frito y frío* (fried and cooled). The excessively strong taste is removed from the oil by frying it for ten or fifteen minutes with an orange or lemon peel and letting it cool off in a well-aired place. Sometimes a quantity of olive oil is prepared in this way and stored in jars for later use. To cut a heavy olive-oil flavor for immediate use, a piece of bread soaked in vinegar or a slice of raw potato can be fried in it for a few minutes before the oil is used. The mere addition of a slice of raw potato during the frying of foods will refine the flavor. However, such methods should be necessary only for poorly refined oil or for delicate pastries. All pure olive oil has at least a slight olive flavor, and when it is good oil, the flavor is an asset to food. Although not traditionally used in Spain, other cooking oils of mild flavor may be substituted for all or a portion of the olive oil called for in any recipe.

Almost as basic as olive oil is garlic. Many arguments could be marshaled in favor of garlic, which the Spaniards consider an aid to digestion as well as a restorative and even a cure for many ills. If you cannot bear the faintest whiff of garlic, some of these recipes are not for you. But first be certain your dislike does not come from eating dishes in which garlic was abused. Garlic in liberal quantities, if absorbed in a slow-cooking sauce, becomes merely one of several factors contributing to the final flavor, and many are the garlic haters who have eagerly devoured a Spanish dish without suspecting garlic as one of its ingredients.

There are many ways of cooking with garlic. The cooking time may be more of a factor than the amount of garlic used. A whole head of garlic cooked in the sauce of a roast, then removed and discarded, will give less of a garlic flavor than one small clove crushed in a salad dressing. In some Spanish recipes, a very subtle flavor is introduced by frying a clove of garlic in olive oil in which meat, fish, or chicken is to be browned; the clove is discarded before the food is fried. Sometimes garlic is roasted in the oven before being added to a sauce, a process which gives it a subtle taste. Sometimes it appears in a sauce, minced and fried, taking on a nutlike flavor. Sometimes two or three cloves are cooked in a sauce whole, unpeeled, and then discarded before the dish is served.

Almonds play an important role in Spanish food. They are used as appetizers, in sauces for meat, fish, and salads, and, above all, in pastry. The Spanish have an extraordinary range of almond cookies, cakes, and candies—for many of which, recipes are given in the dessert section of this book. There is a bewildering variety of almonds available in Spain and even three ways of toasting them. If you can get almonds in the shell, try toasting your own in one of the three ways explained on page 40. It is a little trouble, but highly rewarding.

Casseroles that heat evenly and cook foods slowly are essential for many Spanish dishes. The Spanish use very coarse-grained, inexpensive, fireproof earthenware which comes in all shapes and sizes, from pots 10 inches tall (for cooking beans with sausage, for example) to flat casseroles 7–15 inches in diameter with low or gently sloping sides for rices, stews, and fish dishes. These can all be put directly over a hot flame and very rarely crack. Substitutes are Dutch ovens and heavy cast-iron casseroles and skillets. For the Basque sauces that depend on the blending of olive oil with starch or fish juices at a low temperature, coarse earthware casseroles are by far the most suitable.

The base of countless Spanish sauces is what is known in Spanish as the *sofrito*. The proper cooking of the *sofrito* sometimes determines the quality of the dish, and for this reason, a brief explanation is given here, as well as in recipes using the *sofrito*. A varying quantity of onion is fried in olive oil over a moderate flame until golden; if garlic is used, a chopped clove or two is added when the onion takes on color. When both onion and garlic are golden and soft, peeled chopped tomatoes are added and cooked until the liquid from the tomatoes has evaporated and the sauce has thickened. Seasoned with salt, the *sofrito* is then ready for the addition of the other ingredients called for by the recipe. One of the most common is paprika, always added at low heat or with the pan off the fire to prevent its burning and turning bitter.

28

Many recipes call for the addition of a *picada*. A *picada* is simply two or more ingredients mashed together in a mortar and added to a sauce to flavor or thicken it. The ingredients might be parsley, garlic, and fried bread (often used for thickening instead of flour); or saffron, garlic, and parsley; or almonds and chicken livers. After the *picada* is well ground and mixed, a little of the sauce is added to the mortar to dilute the ground mixture and the contents are then stirred into the sauce. In most cases, an electric blender can do the work in one swift operation.

A peculiarity of Spanish recipes is the occasional use of toasted flour, which is simply flour browned in a slow oven for 10 minutes. Browning eliminates the raw flour taste, and toasted flour is often called for by recipes in which the flour cooks only briefly. Its use is frequent enough for packaged pretoasted flour to be sold in Spain. There are a number of odd combinations of ingredients to be found in certain regional dishes, and some of them, although they sound rather alarming, turn out to be very good. Among the unconventional is the addition of a bit of dark chocolate in the sauce of wild hare, or even a dish of veal chops or fish. The chocolate makes the sauce richer without oversweetening or giving the slightest hint of a chocolate taste. The fish bisque with orange juice from the southern coast does not seem quite so extraordinary if you consider the orange's kinship to lemon, so commonly used with fish, and the orange flavor is actually delicious (see recipe on p. 69). At the use of blood pudding in a dessert, however, I have drawn the line, and you will not find a recipe for the *jayuelas* of Asturia. In any case, these oddities are the exception, not the rule of Spanish cooking, which in general is sober and classical.

29

SPANISH WINES

Wine is always served with meals in Spain. The poorest peasant is more apt to be short of water than wine, and mineral water often costs more than wine in shops and restaurants. As in all Latin countries, alcohol is primarily a complement to food: wine with a meal; wine or sherry before the meal to prepare the palate; sweet wine, sweet sherry, or cognac after a meal to aid digestion.

The ordinary, unbottled wine served in Spanish restaurants and drunk in the homes is truly a regional wine, unlike the so-called regional wines of some areas, which so often contain a goodly admixture of strong, imported wine of poor quality. Some Spanish wines are excellent, some are too coarse, some too sweet, but the existence of regional wines as well as regional foods adds to the pleasure and adventure of travel in Spain. Unfortunately, traveling is the only way to enjoy some of the most delectable of all Spanish wines: the green wines of Galicia and the Basque country, which are made from partly unripened grapes and do not withstand transport even to other parts of Spain.

Spain is the world's third producer of wine and its inhabitants are used to having a generous supply. Even when European vineyards were decimated at the end of the nineteenth century, a British consul in southern Spain reported that wine was so abundant it was mixed with cement during a drought. For lack of rainfall, Spain produces less wine per acre than France, but, for the same reason, the wine produced is of higher alcoholic content. The sugar content of a grape is directly related to the amount of heat it receives, and it is the sugar in wine that turns wholly or in part into alcohol. Therefore the sweetest and most alcoholic wines are grown in hot countries (although south of the Canary Islands, the heat becomes too intense to permit wine production because the sun dries the grape before it matures). Non-fortified Spanish wines range in alcoholic content from 9 percent in the Burgos area (an exceptional low) to 18 percent or more in the south and on the Mediterranean coast.

Wine producing has a venerable history in Spain; the Phoenicians are believed to have planted the first vines approximately 3,000 years ago. Spain has been exporting wine since Roman times and now ships to ninety-eight countries, not including Spanish possessions overseas. In bottled wines, sherry leads the list, with the Rioja wines following second. Switzerland and Great Britain are the top consumers by far, followed by Germany, Belgium-Luxemburg, Austria, Holland, Sweden, Denmark, Hungary, and the U.S.A., which takes fifteen years to consume what Switzerland imports annually.

It is unfortunate that bottled Spanish wines are relatively little known in North America. They can be extremely good and they are the best possible accompaniment for Spanish foods. Of the bottled wines imported to the U.S.A., dry table wines and sherries predominate. It is interesting to note from the statistics of the official Spanish wine syndicate (Sindicato de la Vid) that the dry wines of Córdoba, described later in this section, are sold in the U.S.A., as well as sparkling wines from the cellars of Barcelona and Villafranca del Panadés. The Rioja wines predominate among table wines, as one might expect: they are the best bottled Spanish table wines, and there are great wines among them. Unlike some Spanish wines, the Riojas age beautifully and travel very well.

There are vineyards all over Spain, each producing a wine of distinct character. In a brief survey, one would have to mention the unexportable and giddy *chacolí* of the Basque country and the *caldos* of Galicia, which also produces a wine similar to port; the fine rosés of Navarre, the dry virile wines of Aragon, the rich and potent *priorato* and the pleasant, light white wines and sparkling wines of Catalonia; the wines of Alicante and Valencia whose suavity masks strong alcoholic content, and the quantity-producing vineyards of La Mancha, whose wines cannot be aged.

The Rioja area is a fertile valley following the River Ebro between the Cantabrian Mountains and the Castilian Sierra. Wine growing has long been taken very seriously in the Rioja, so much so that in 1635, the authorities of the producing center of Logroño even forbade all vehicle traffic in the city on the grounds that it disturbed the wine aging in the casks. Eight types of grape are grown: four for red and four for white. From these, a great variety of wines is elaborated by the twenty-four registered Rioja producers, from the Herededores del Marqués de Riscal, which make only one wine (of the same name), an excellent light, dry red wine always aged four years before it is sold, to the Bodegas Bilbaínas, which produce twenty wines: white, red, rosé, and sparkling, ranging from dry to sweet in the whites, each bearing its own label according to its age and characteristics. There are wines for every taste in the Rioja, but probably the best of all are the rich red wines, often compared to Bordeaux.

The South is the area of perfumed wines, of which the most famous is sherry, a wine almost in a class by itself.

The province of Córdoba also produces distinctive, somewhat sherrylike wines, *montilla* and *moriles,* both grown
near the city of Montilla. (The term *amontillado* has been
adopted for certain sherries which have some of the
characteristics of *montilla.*) Málaga has special portlike
wines; one of the best known is Lacrima Christi, a dessert
wine.

The English name *sherry* probably comes from the
name the Moors gave the town now known as Jerez de la
Frontera: *Sherisch.* The town was called Xera by the
Greeks and is thought to have been founded by the
Phoenicians around 1100 B.C., although not necessarily on
the site on which it stands today. Wines have been
exported from this area for hundreds of years. England has
been buying sherry (or "sack") since the twelfth century.
Surprisingly enough, it was only in the nineteenth century
that sherry began to be exported in bottles.

Sherry is not one wine but a gamut of wines, all
produced in a tiny corner of southern Spain near Portugal.
To be called sherry, the wine must be grown within the
province of Cádiz and elaborated according to specific
regulations by registered producers within a triangle
formed by the cities Jerez de la Frontera, Sanlúcar de
Barrameda, and Puerto de Santa María. Because soil and
climate are the dominating factors in the creation of
sherry, it has proved impossible to produce it anywhere
else in the world. Vines grown for sherry and transplanted
to California and the Rhineland have produced wine
totally unlike sherry in both places. Vines transplanted
from other parts of Spain to the sherry area for the
production of table wines have produced sherry-type wines
instead. The vines of the sherry area of Spain were
replaced by California plants after the epidemic of phyl-

loxera in 1894 destroyed European vineyards. Grafted, the vines are now producing wine of the same character and quality as before; the only change is the reduction of their productive life from 50–70 years to 15–20.

The soil of the sherry area is of three kinds. The most characteristic and best is an almost white, chalky soil which does not crack in the blazing sun, thus allowing the roots of the vines to retain moisture through the summer. Chalk in soil is highly valued and found in areas of great vineyards: in Cognac Grande-Champagne, the soil contains 50 percent to 75 percent chalk; in the sherry area, it contains up to 80 percent. There is also a clay soil which produces fairly good wines, and a sandy soil which yields twice the quantity, but an inferior quality.

The hot sun and lack of rainfall contribute to the high alcoholic content; the sea winds (and all winds in this corner of Spain are from either the Mediterranean or the Atlantic) are believed to influence the flavor of the grape and of the wine while it matures in casks. It is said that the flavor varies according to the direction the vats face in the cellar.

The elaboration and maturing of sherry is different from the processes used for other wines and is designed to maintain the character of the distinct types from year to year. After harvest in September, the grapes are put on round mats for a day to dry in the sun. Covered at night for protection against the humidity, they are then pressed and the juice is allowed to ferment violently during one week. A period of slow fermentation follows, lasting until December or January, when the experts make the first of many classifications. Wines from the same kind of grape picked the same day in the same area are already found to vary, and the experts put a chalk mark on each barrel to assign the wine to one of four categories; the fourth category is condemned to use as commercial alcohol. Many more tests are made before the classification is definitive because the wines are not considered fully stable until they are three years old.

The fermented wine is drawn out of the barrels into clean casks to separate it from the residue and is fortified to a minimum strength of 15.5 percent and generally to 17 or 18 percent alcohol. The casks, each of which holds over 100 gallons, are stacked in three, four, or in rare cases, five tiers in cellars built entirely above ground in the higher and drier parts of the three towns where sherry is elaborated. Each barrel is only one-third full in order to give the wine oxygen, and in the spring the casks are left loosely corked or covered with tiles instead of corks to encourage the growth of the yeast that gives sherry some of its inimitable character.

Sherry is a long-lived wine. Twelve years is an ideal age, although much older wines are used in blends. It is in the above ground cellars called "bodegas" that the wines are aged, but while aging, they are frequently mixed with older wines. This process, peculiar to sherry making, is called the *solera* system. Its purpose is to obtain a final product with the same qualities bottle after bottle, year after year. Wine for bottling and delivery is drawn from the bottom, or oldest, barrel. The liquid removed is replaced from the next tier, or the next-to-oldest barrel, which, in turn, is filled to the same level from the next tier, and so forth. Withdrawals are made two or three times a year in quantities determined by the demand, but the barrels must always contain a preponderance of old wine. To ensure this, the cellar has to maintain stocks at least five times larger than its annual sales. Some bodegas have as many as 8,000 casks.

The varieties of sherry are too numerous to be listed. There are close to two hundred producers permitted to use the label "sherry," and each makes his own sherries, his own blends. Only by experimenting and remembering both the name of the sherry and the name of the producer will you find the sherries you prefer. The basic types of sherries are as follows:

fino: very pale topaz, very dry, with from 15 to 17 percent alcohol.

amontillado: amber in color, light and dry, with a pungent aroma and a somewhat nutlike flavor. Normally 16–18 percent alcohol, but if very old, may reach 20–24 percent.

oloroso: has a strong bouquet, a nutlike flavor, more body than *amontillado,* and is a dark gold, sometimes reddish color. Basically dry, it leaves an aftertaste of sweetness. Eighteen to 20 percent alcohol is the norm, although with age, an *oloroso* may contain 24–25 percent.

Pedro Ximénez and *Moscatel:* sweet dessert wines, named after the sweet grapes from which they are obtained. The grapes are exposed to the sun for fifteen to twenty days after harvest to increase the sugar content. Both wines are sold bottled and are used in blends such as cream sherries and *abocados.*

manzanilla: a new wine that appeared at the beginning of the nineteenth century, it is produced in the white chalk soils near Sanlúcar de Barrameda, and is aged in dark humid sites aired by Atlantic breezes (some bodegas have windows opening directly on the sea).

Its special characteristics appear when it is four years old; aged longer, it passes its prime.

Sangría is listed on menus and winecards throughout Spain. A kind of punch, it is a popular Spanish drink often served with appetizers and even throughout a meal. Many people put in it various fruits, spices, or hard liquors, and let it macerate 24 hours or more. According to the representative of one of the largest wine houses in Spain, the true *Sangría,* for those who like wine, is made fresh, served iced, and contains:

> *a bottle of red wine, dry and full-bodied*
> *the juice of a lemon*
> *a sliced lemon*
> *sparkling water to taste*

For those who prefer a mixture, the following is an excellent one, best made the day before and served very cold:

> *a bottle of dry red wine*
> *a glass of cognac*
> *a dash of curaçao*
> *sugar to taste*
> *sparkling water to taste* (*optional*)

CHAPTER 2

TAPAS (APPETIZERS)

THE serving of tapas is one of the very pleasant customs of Spain and a specialty of Madrid, which is responsible for the widespread popularity if not the invention of the idea. Tapas may be nothing more than toasted almonds and olives, but some bars and restaurants offer an extraordinarily extensive variety of tapas, many of them small portions of dishes suitable for a first or even a main course.

Tapas are available everywhere in Spain. A laborer can have a few mussels or snails or clams with his glass of wine after work in the humblest bar, and the fish served will be irreproachably fresh. In Madrid, bars, taverns, and restaurants that specialize in tapas offer thirty choices or more. Between 8 and 10 P.M., these places are filled with people, most of them standing and all of them eating with toothpicks from little oval dishes while drinking wine or sherry. Some people end by going from one bar to another and altogether skip sitting down to a proper meal. How easy it is to do so can be seen in a glance at the tapas offered. For example, the menu at the Gayango, a popular spot for tapas in Madrid, lists scallops, grilled prawns, garlic shrimp, seafood cocktail, pickled herring, Soldaditos de Pavía (fried codsticks), roast veal, ham, mushroom casserole, smoked salmon, the miniature fresh anchovies from Málaga known as *chanquetes,* and sausages. There are also *palitos,* long toothpicks laden with smoked anchovy, ham, cheese, foie-gras, smoked trout, or smoked eel; *pinchos,* metal skewers 4–5 inches long on which mushrooms or kidneys have been broiled; and tiny sandwiches of everything from smoked orange duck to cheese.

Some of these require hours of preparation or individual serving dishes, but others offer new ideas for cocktail tidbits quickly made and easily served. Even the conventional olives and nuts can present a surprising variety.

OLIVES AND NUTS

OLIVES

When raw olives are put in brine in Spain, herbs, spices, or peppers are often added to flavor them. Although the raw fruit absorbs seasoning more readily, flavoring can be added to olives purchased in cans or jars too. Keep a quantity of olives in a glass jar and let them steep in their own brine with hot peppers or garlic (or both), or lemon and orange peel. When buying olives, look for diversity: small black ones, deep green, olive green, or light green ones of different sizes; olives stuffed with anchovy, with pimiento, with lemon peel—there is an infinite gamut of olives.

TOASTED ALMONDS

Toasting your own almonds takes time, but is highly rewarding; the result bears little resemblance to canned or packaged nuts. Shelled almonds can be toasted in large batches and kept fresh for weeks in tightly closed glass jars. There are three classic ways of toasting almonds (described below) and the three flavors are distinct.

First method: The easiest way to toast almonds is in the shell, to be cracked and opened by the consumers. The almonds are simply placed in a preheated low oven (about 275°) for 30–45 minutes or until toasted through. The pan should be shaken occasionally to ensure even toasting. The only way to determine whether the nuts are done is to crack one open and eat it. They must be tested frequently when almost roasted because they can turn black inside without giving any outward sign of burning.

Second method: Crack the shells and toast the almonds without removing the brown peel that encloses the nut. Roast 30–45 minutes in a 275° oven. Shake up from time to time during roasting. The almonds are done when the skin slips off easily between the fingers.

Third method: This is the most delicious and also the longest. After the almonds are removed from the hard shell, they are scalded and peeled. To scald, put almonds in boiling water off the fire for ½ minute or until the almond slips out of its skin easily when squeezed between the fingers. Strain almonds, rinse under cold water, and peel at once. Toast as in the preceding recipe.

GLAZED ALMONDS

To glaze, rub scalded, peeled, and toasted almonds in a little olive oil while the nuts are still warm from the oven;

then sprinkle with salt. The salt will form a crust when dry.

FRIED ALMONDS

Scalded (see toasted almonds, third method, above) and peeled, the almonds are fried in enough olive oil to cover the bottom of the skillet. The oil should be only moderately hot in order to permit the nuts to cook through without burning outside. Stir frequently while cooking. Drain, salt, and serve.

TOASTED OR FRIED PINE NUTS

Washed, drained, salted, and toasted in a moderate oven or fried in enough moderately hot olive oil to cover the bottom of a skillet, pine nuts make an exquisite tapa, warm or cold.

TOASTED HAZELNUTS

Like toasted almonds, these can be kept fresh in a tightly closed glass jar for weeks. Remove shells, but not brown skin. Toast in a 275° oven for 25–30 minutes or until the nut tastes roasted and the skin comes off easily. Put nuts in a kitchen towel and rub to remove skin. Serve salted or not as you prefer.

CANAPÉS

The quickest canapés are those made with foods that need no more preparation than being cut into bits and put on squares of toast. A few suggestions are: cheese, cured ham, *chorizo* sausage, smoked trout, smoked eel, smoked salmon, canned sardines, and rolled or flat fillets of canned anchovy. To decorate, use chopped cured ham, chopped or sliced black and green olives, chopped hard-boiled egg, minced parsley, bits of tomato or canned pimiento, capers, and truffles. A dab of sauce such as All-i-oli (pp. 188–191) or Romesco (p. 193) will transform cold meat canapés. Canapé spreads can be made rapidly from canned or precooked foods as in the following:

CANAPÉ OF PURÉED SARDINE

Remove bones from canned sardine, mash fish in mortar, spread on toast, and decorate with chopped hard-boiled egg.

CANAPÉ OF PURÉED TUNA

Mash tuna in mortar with yolks of hard-boiled egg and mix with mayonnaise until it spreads easily on toast.

CANAPÉ OF PURÉED CHICKEN

Crush leftover chicken meat in a mortar with a few toasted almonds, season with salt and white pepper, and add sherry until the paste has the desired consistency. Serve on toast.

CANAPÉ OF PURÉED HAKE

Use leftover cooked hake or simmer a slice of fresh fish until cooked through (5–10 minutes). Any white fish may be substituted for hake. When fish is cool, mash with a fork, mix with a little mayonnaise, season with salt and pepper to taste, and spread on toast. Sprinkle with chopped hard-boiled egg.

42

Whole fillets of small fish make delicious canapés. Any small, flat fish, such as young flounder, may be substituted for sole in the following recipe.

CANAPÉ OF BABY SOLE

Wash cleaned soles, cover with cold water, and bring to a boil. Reduce flame and let fish simmer until cooked through (a very few minutes). When fish has cooled, carefully cut out the fillets, put them on strips of toast, and decorate with capers.

BANDERILLAS

Banderillas (also known as *palitos*) are long toothpicks laden with bits of colorfully combined delicacies. For example, a banderilla might be made up of pickled vegetables (carrot, cauliflower, and onion) alternated with slices of hot pickled peppers and pitted green olives. Anything that can be threaded on a toothpick and eaten with cocktails can be used. Some of the foods suitable for banderillas are ham, cheese, smoked fish (trout, eel, salmon), capers, anchovies, pitted olives, shrimp, mussels, clams, pimiento, sausages, and cold meats.

FRITOS (FRIED APPETIZERS)

Fried appetizers are served warm or hot in bite-size pieces to be eaten with toothpicks. Shellfish are particularly popular: clams, mussels, shrimp, and scallops. Some of these can be partially prepared in advance.

FRIED CLAMS

Rinse small fresh clams under running water and soak 1 hour in a bowl of cool water to eliminate sand. Drain and put in a pan with enough white wine to cover bottom of pan to depth of ½ inch. Season wine with ground pepper. Heat over moderate fire until clams open. Shake pan occasionally during cooking so that the shellfish heat evenly. Once all have opened, allow them to cool in the liquid. (All the preceding can be done hours before you plan to serve.)

Remove meat from shells, roll in flour, dip in beaten egg, and fry in hot olive oil deep enough to cover the shellfish. Serve hot on toothpicks.

FRIED MUSSELS

Substitute mussels for clams in the above recipe. See page 115 for cleaning of mussels.

FRIED SHRIMP

Cook shrimp for 3 minutes in boiling salted water. Strain, let cool, and remove shell. With a knife, remove the alimentary canal or black line along the back of the shrimp. (This much can be done hours in advance.)

Shortly before serving, roll shrimp in flour, dip in beaten egg, and fry in enough hot olive oil to cover the shrimp.

FRIED SCALLOPS

Remove scallops from their shells, cut in slices, dip in dry bread crumbs, then in beaten egg, and fry in enough hot olive oil to cover the scallops.

FRIED CLAMS IN THE SHELL

These can be prepared in 2–3 minutes (after the clams have been rinsed and soaked in a bowl of cool water for 1 hour to eliminate sand). Small clams are best for this recipe.

Drain clams and fry in a small quantity of hot olive oil (just enough to cover the bottom of the skillet). Sprinkle clams with salt as you fry and remove them as soon as all are open. They are delicious eaten off the shell, but you can remove the meat and serve it on toothpicks if you prefer. Serve hot.

PINCHOS

A *pincho* is broiled food, usually meat or mushrooms, cooked and served on a short metal skewer (4–5 inches long). Cubes of meat are sometimes alternated with button mushrooms or bits of onion or red pepper. Mushrooms alone are good, as are chicken livers, marinated in olive oil for 1 hour before grilling. Tender lamb cut in small bits and basted with olive oil is delicious.

BUÑUELITOS (SMALL FRITTERS)

Fritters take about ½ hour to prepare, but because the batter can be made beforehand (even the previous day), there is little work at the last minute. The fritters should be small enough to be eaten in one bite from a toothpick. They need not be served hot, and in fact are best just warm. The following batter, which will make three to four dozen small fritters, can be used for many varieties.

45

FRITTER BATTER

⅓ cup flour   1 egg
⅓ tsp baking powder   ⅓ cup water

Put flour in mixing bowl and gradually add enough water (about ⅓ cup) to make a batter of the consistency of a thin cream sauce. Stir in one lightly beaten egg and the baking powder.

BUÑUELITOS DE BACALAO
(COD FRITTERS)

1 well-packed cup of de-   2 TB chopped parsley
    salted cod (see p.   1 recipe Fritter Batter
    115)   (see above)
2 medium cloves garlic,   ½ cup olive oil for fry-
    peeled   ing
               salt to taste

Shred cod with fingers. Chop well with garlic and parsley. Add to batter, stir, and salt to taste. (This much may be done a day in advance.)

Heat enough olive oil in a large frying pan to cover the bottom to a depth of ¼ inch (about ½ cup). When oil begins to smoke, drop in cod mixture off teaspoon and fry until well browned, turning once. Total frying time will be 10–15 minutes. Drain on brown paper before serving.

NOTE: The finer you shred and chop the cod, the smoother the fritters will be. However, some prefer fritters with coarse flakes of cod. It is entirely a matter of taste.

BUÑUELITOS DE JAMON
(HAM FRITTERS)

¾ cup cured ham, minced	1 recipe Fritter Batter (p. 46)
1 small onion, chopped fine	½ cup olive oil for frying
salt to taste	

Fry the minced ham in 2 TB olive oil. When ham is browned, remove it and fry chopped onion until golden brown. When ham and onion have cooled, add them to fritter batter along with any oil left in frying pan. Salt to taste. (This part may be prepared the day before.) Fry fritters as directed in the preceding recipe.

BUÑUELITOS DE HUEVO DURO
(HARD-BOILED-EGG FRITTERS)

4 hard-boiled eggs	½ cup olive oil for frying
1 slice cured ham, minced	salt and pepper
1 recipe Fritter Batter (p. 46)	

Chop hard-boiled eggs, mince ham, mix in batter, add salt and pepper to taste, and fry as in recipe for Cod Fritters.

BUÑUELITOS DE POLLO
(CHICKEN FRITTERS)

1 cup cooked chicken, minced	½ cup olive oil for frying
1 recipe Fritter Batter	salt and pepper

47

Add minced chicken to batter, season with salt and pepper, and fry as directed in recipe for Cod Fritters.

EMPANADILLAS (SMALL PASTRIES)

Little cocktail pastries are excellent made with any leftover, unsweetened dough. Fresh dough does not take long to prepare and can be mixed the day before if you wish. For that matter, the pastries can be baked hours in advance. Best hot or warmed over in a moderate oven, they are also good cold. The following recipe makes enough dough for about forty bite-size pastries or thirty tartlets.

EMPANADILLA DOUGH

1½ cups flour	2 TB olive oil
1 egg	1 tsp baking powder
2 TB milk	1 tsp salt

Put flour on a board or marble slab, make a hole in the center, add all the ingredients in the hole, and mix well with fingers. Roll into a ball and cover with a damp cloth. The dough must rest for 15 minutes before use; it can be kept in a cool place for 24 hours.

EMPANADILLAS DE CHORIZO
(CHORIZO PASTRIES)

1 slender chorizo (or pepperoni) sausage cut in about 40 slices	1 raw egg yolk
	1 recipe Empanadilla Dough

Preheat oven to 400°. Divide dough in two. Roll out half; place sausage slices on rolled dough, pressing them down slightly. Roll out other half of dough and put it over the sausages. Using a cookie cutter or a thin-edged glass, cut out a circle around each sausage slice large enough to leave a margin of dough around the sausage. Pinch the edges of the two halves together, brush tops with beaten egg yolk diluted in a little water, prick pastries with a fork, and bake in 400° oven 15–20 minutes or until browned.

EMPANADILLAS DE JAMON
(*HAM PASTRIES*)

Cut bite-size pieces from a thick slice of cured or smoked ham and substitute for the *chorizo* in the preceding recipe.

NOTE: You can stuff the pastries with cubes of leftover roast, bits of cooked chicken, hash, fried pork sausage, or any filling you choose.

TARTALETAS

Open-faced tartlets are even more versatile than empanadillas. They can be made from the same dough and the shells can be baked hours in advance. The filling should be added no more than an hour before serving. There is a variety of cold foods suitable for fillings. Some suggestions are red caviar; anchovy with chopped hard-boiled egg; chopped chicken with mayonnaise; chopped tuna with mayonnaise and minced green olives; fish, fresh or canned, with mayonnaise and capers; cold vegetable salad with chopped cured ham. The tartlets take the form of boats in the sample recipe below, but they can be given any shape you wish: oblong, square, or round. Regardless of the shape, the baking of the shells is the same as in the following recipe.

BARCOS DE ANCHOAS A LA SEVILLANA
(*SEVILLIAN ANCHOVY BOATS*)

1 recipe Empanadilla Dough
2 small cans of pimiento
2 cans of rolled anchovies

yolk of 1 hard-boiled egg
ground black pepper
rice for baking tarts

Preheat oven to 375°. Roll out dough, form small boats, prick bottoms in 2 or 3 places with a knife. Fill boats with raw rice to make them keep their hollow shape during baking. Bake in 375° oven for about 10 minutes or until firm. Discard rice.

Shortly before serving, dice pimiento, soak it in the liquid from the cans of anchovy and season it with ground black pepper. Fill boats with the pimiento, sprinkle tops with a little mashed yolk of hard-boiled egg, and decorate with rolled anchovy.

CHAPTER 3

SALADS AND ENTREMESES (HORS D'OEUVRES)

SALAD is a first course in Spain as it is in California, where the custom may be a legacy of the Conquistadores. Salad is sometimes simply lettuce and tomato; sometimes it includes a number of vegetables. The Spanish rarely make a tossed salad. Instead, they arrange the vegetables decoratively on a large shallow platter and sprinkle the whole generously with salt, olive oil, and wine vinegar, or just olive oil and salt. Small slender-spouted cruets of vinegar and olive oil are put on the table for those who want more seasoning. The most decorative salads are probably those made by the Catalans. The greens and reds of the peppers, tomatoes, and lettuce, the blacks and

51

greens of the olives, and the white rings of onion lend themselves to innumerable appetizing patterns.

Salad may be served alone or accompanied by a few slices of cold sausage or ham. When there are many accompanying tidbits, the salad is reduced in size and variety, and the collection of platters is called *entremeses variados* (assorted hors d'oeuvres). These can be as rich or as simple as you choose; they can even constitute a full meal as in a typical Catalan dish called Xató, whose recipe is given on page 55.

ENSALADA CATALANA
(*CATALAN SALAD*)

The basic ingredients of a summer salad are:

romaine or curly endive lettuce, washed, dried, separated into leaves, and broken into manageable size. This forms the bed of the salad
tomatoes cut in slices or quarters
sweet raw onion cut in thin rings or slices. (If the onion is very strong, it is soaked in vinegar and water for an hour before serving to reduce sharpness)
green and red peppers cut in thin rings
green and black olives

Optional additions (or winter substitutes) are:

radishes, whole or sliced
celery stalk, cubed
hard-boiled eggs in rings or quarters

For a more substantial first dish, the salad may be dotted with bits of canned tuna or shreds of desalted cod fish. It may be surrounded by slices of sausage or accompanied by side platters containing a few sliced hams and sausages. The salad is sprinkled liberally with olive oil; lightly with vinegar and salt.

ENSALADA MADRILEÑA
(MADRID SALAD)

SERVINGS: 6

1 *large head of lettuce*
4 *medium tomatoes*
2 *hard-boiled eggs*
olive oil
wine vinegar

6–7 *pitted black olives per person*
6 *or more small marinated fishes (pp.* 57–58)

salt to taste

Peel tomatoes, squeeze out seeds, and chop fine. Mix with chopped lettuce, olives, and fish, boned and chopped. Season with olive oil, vinegar, and salt (or oil and vinegar dressing, p. 54). Top with slices of hard-boiled eggs.

ENSALADA MURCIANA
(MURCIAN SALAD)

SERVINGS: 6

2 *medium heads of lettuce (preferably romaine or Boston)*
2 *medium green peppers*
2 *medium cucumbers*
3 *large tomatoes*

½ *medium onion (preferably a sweet, mild onion)*
9 TB *olive oil*
3 TB *vinegar*
½ *tsp salt*

Dice washed lettuce, peppers, tomatoes, onions, and peeled cucumbers, but keep them all separate. Put a layer

53

of chopped lettuce in a flat-bottomed serving dish with fairly high sides. Cover with a layer of chopped pepper, then a layer of cucumbers, topped by the onions and, lastly, the tomatoes. Mix olive oil, vinegar, and salt in a bowl and pour it over the salad. Cover the dish and keep it in a cool place for at least 2 hours before serving. Serve in the dish in which it was made.

ENSALADA SEVILLANA
(SEVILLIAN SALAD)

SERVINGS: 6

1 large head curly endive

3–4 branches fresh tarragon

7–8 pitted olives per person

oil and vinegar dressing (see below)

Wash curly endive and dry thoroughly. Toss with pitted olives and chopped leaves of tarragon in oil and vinegar dressing.

OIL AND VINEGAR DRESSING
SERVINGS: enough for 1 large head of lettuce

3 generous TB *olive oil   a large pinch of salt*

1 scant TB *wine vinegar*

Pour olive oil into a bowl. Add salt and stir vigorously until it forms a thick, cloudy sauce. Stir in vinegar.

For a strong garlic flavor add a crushed clove of garlic to the olive oil. If you are making a tossed salad, mix dressing directly in salad bowl. For a light taste of garlic, rub sides of bowl with a garlic clove before making the dressing.

54

XATÓ

SERVINGS: 6

Xató (pronounced *cha-toh'*) is a Catalan dish traditionally eaten in January and February, the two coldest months, during which the Catalans find the sharp taste stimulating and warming, although they ordinarily use very little pepper in their food. It is during this season, too, that the heart of curly endive, which is the base of the dish, is whitest. Generally served as a first course in Catalonia, Xató is substantial enough to constitute a supper or lunch.

For Xató, take curly endive in quantity (two very large heads for six people), separate the leaves, and soak them in Xató sauce for at least an hour in advance of the meal. Serve the salad in a large bowl, accompanied by platters of cured ham, a variety of cold sausages, fillets of anchovy, white bean omelet (p. 85), and marinated fish (pp. 57–58).

XATÓ SAUCE

3 *cloves garlic*
7–8 *peeled and toasted almonds*
1 *or more sharp chili peppers (or pow-dered cayenne pepper)*
½ *cup olive oil*
¼ *cup wine vinegar*
¾ *tsp salt*

This sauce can be made in 5 minutes in an electric blender: simply put all the ingredients in at once and beat until the pepper is reduced to fine particles. If you do not have a blender, crush the garlic and almonds in a mortar, add one or more finely chopped chili peppers, and mash to

55

a smooth paste before gradually blending in the oil and vinegar. The number of peppers (or the amount of cayenne) you use depends on how sharp you like the sauce. When tasting for seasoning, bear in mind that the sauce will seem less sharp when mixed with the salad.

ENTREMESES VARIADOS
(*ASSORTED HORS D'OEUVRES*)

Entremeses variados can include any of the dishes listed under tapas plus small portions of more substantial foods which, served in quantity, would be suitable for a first or even a main course. The usual *entremeses variados,* however, are limited to the following items, presented on serving platters or distributed in advance on each person's plate:

three or four varieties of cold sausages
a slice per person of cured ham
a dish of anchovy fillets
a dish of canned tuna
at least two varieties of olives
a small platter of salad greens and tomatoes, seasoned with vinegar, olive oil, and salt

The classic *entremeses variados* may also include:

Artichoke Hearts in Oil
Escalivada (p. 221)
Cold Mussels with Almond Sauce (p. 116) or Tomato Sauce (p. 117)
Boiled Fresh Shrimp with All-i-oli (pp. 189–190)

Cod Croquettes (p. 128)
Raw, Shredded, Desalted Codfish in Olive Oil
Squid a la Romana (p. 125)
Small Marinated Fish (see following recipes)

PESCADITOS EN ESCABECHE A LA CATALANA
(*SMALL MARINATED FISH CATALAN STYLE*)
SERVINGS: 12 small fish

12 small fresh fish	*a pinch of cayenne*
(mackerel,* anchovy,	*pepper*
or sardine)	*½ head garlic, un-*
¼ cup olive oil for fry-	*peeled*
ing	*few sprigs parsley,*
1 cup olive oil for mari-	*chopped*
nade	*½ tsp black pepper*
1 TB paprika	*salt to taste*
flour for dusting	

Fry lightly floured fish in ¼ cup olive oil over medium
heat. When lightly browned put in a recipient, preferably
one with a flat surface large enough to accommodate the
fish. Heat the cup of olive oil over a high flame. Fry in it a
coarsely chopped, unpeeled half head of garlic with the
black pepper and chopped parsley. Let it bubble, stir a few
times, remove pan from fire, and blend in the paprika
mixed with the cayenne. Add salt to taste. Pour the hot
liquid over the fish. Let it marinate 24 hours before
serving. The fish will keep in a cool place five days or
more.

* With mackerel, it is preferable to use only the fillets, which
you can remove from the fish after it is browned.

PESCADITOS EN ESCABECHE A LA ANDALUZA
(SMALL MARINATED FISH ANDALUSIAN STYLE)

SERVINGS: 12 small fish

12 small fresh fish (mackerel * or anchovy)	*½ tsp cumin seed*
	¼ tsp ginger
	⅓ cup vinegar
¼ cup olive oil for frying	*⅔ cup water*
	½ lemon sliced
2 medium cloves garlic	*2 bay leaves*
a pinch of saffron	*salt to taste*

flour for dusting

Fry lightly floured fish in ¼ cup olive oil over medium heat. When lightly browned put in a recipient, preferably one with a flat surface large enough to accommodate the fish. Crush the garlic, saffron, cumin seed, and ginger in a mortar. Stir in the vinegar and water, salt to taste, and cover the fishes with the mixture. Put in half a sliced lemon and two bay leaves. Let it marinate 24 hours before serving. This dish will keep for several days in a cool place.

* With mackerel, it is preferable to use only the fillets, which you can remove from the fish after browning.

CHAPTER 4

GAZPACHO

TYPICAL of La Mancha and Andalusia, there are some thirty classic versions and many variations of this ancient dish. Gazpacho is quite unknown in the north of Spain, and my first hint of it in Catalonia came through a new maid from Estremadura. I had left her in charge of preparing lunch and given explicit instructions for the washing and drying of the salad greens: they were to be shaken, hung for at least an hour to drain, and then wiped one by one in a towel before being put in the bowl in which I had already mixed the dressing. When I returned to the house at lunchtime and stopped in the kitchen to ask if everything was ready, the maid replied that all that lacked was the finishing touch to the salad, for which she had awaited my arrival. At that, she brought out the bowl of carefully dried salad greens and, before my astonished and horrified eyes, poured a pitcher of ice water into it. It was only after I became familiar with gazpacho that I

59

began to understand why.

Gazpacho is not always liquid, however, nor is it always iced, nor does it always contain tomatoes. Because it is served in so many forms and such diverse ways, from first to middle to last course, or throughout the meal as a beverage, it belongs in a category of its own. The peasant gazpacho is a noonday meal, prepared in the fields in a wooden bowl and eaten directly from the bowl with wooden spoons. It might be a rather liquid dish like Gazpacho Sevillano, whose recipe is given below, or a thicker one like the Salmorejo, which sometimes contains hard-boiled eggs. Gazpacho Blanco, composed of only olive oil, vinegar, water, garlic, and almonds, is more of a refreshing drink; it is typical of Córdoba. The Gazpacho Extremeño (of Estremadura) also omits the cucumber and tomato of Andalusia. It is made with bread, garlic, vinegar, green pepper, a raw egg, olive oil, salt, and water. In Madrid, gazpacho is made only in the hottest summer months and contains cumin seeds. Gazpachuelo, a derivative of gazpacho, starts with a mayonnaise base and in its humblest versions has nothing more than mayonnaise, water, lemon, and either boiled potatoes or rice. A good gazpachuelo from Málaga, however, becomes a delicious kind of fish soup (p. 64).

GAZPACHO SEVILLANO
(*SEVILLIAN GAZPACHO*)

SERVINGS: 4

1 small clove garlic, peeled	*¼ small cucumber*
¼ small green pepper	*6 TB olive oil*
½ small onion	*2 TB wine vinegar*
2 large ripe tomatoes	*4 cups ice water*
	salt to taste

If you use a mortar, crush garlic, pepper cut in strips, onion, and salt. Add tomato and cucumber and mash. Stir in oil gradually. Mix in vinegar. Strain into deep bowl. Pour in 4 cups ice water, season with salt, mix well, and serve very cold.

If you use an electric blender, mix all ingredients except water simultaneously. Blend on low speed for only a few seconds, then strain and proceed as described above.

NOTE: Diced cucumber and green pepper, grated hard-boiled egg, chopped tomato, and cubed toast or stale bread may be served apart for each person to sprinkle over the soup.

GAZPACHO ANDALUZ
(ANDALUSIAN GAZPACHO)

SERVINGS: 4

3 large ripe tomatoes, coarsely chopped

2 green peppers, seeded and sliced

1 clove garlic, peeled

5 TB olive oil

2 TB wine vinegar

white part of 2 slices of bread

4 cups ice water

1½ slices toasted bread, cubed

salt to taste

If you use a mortar, crush garlic with peppers and a little salt. Add chopped tomatoes and bread previously soaked in water and squeezed. When this is well mixed, gradually add olive oil while blending. Mix in ½ cup water when the oil is completely absorbed. Pass through a sieve into a deep recipient, add vinegar and 3½ cups ice water, season with salt to taste, and serve with cubes of toasted bread on top or in a bowl on the side.

61

GAZPACHO

If you use an electric blender, mix all ingredients simultaneously except water and cubes of toast. Blend on low speed for only a few seconds, then strain. Add water, check seasoning, and serve as described above.

GAZPACHO MADRILEÑO
(GAZPACHO OF MADRID)

SERVINGS: 4

3 green peppers, seeded and sliced
2 ripe medium-sized tomatoes, coarsely chopped
2 ripe medium-sized tomatoes, cubed
1 clove garlic, peeled

5 TB olive oil
3½ cups ice water
1 small cucumber
2 slices of day-old white bread cut in cubes
2 TB wine vinegar
¼ tsp cumin seed

salt to taste

If you use a mortar, crush garlic with two of the peppers, a little salt, and the cumin seed. Add the coarsely chopped tomatoes and mix well. Gradually add olive oil. Mix in ½ cup water when the olive oil is completely absorbed. Pass through a sieve into a deep recipient. Stir in 3 cups ice water; season with salt to taste. Serve in individual bowls topped with slices of peeled cucumber, the remaining green pepper in slices, the cubed tomatoes, and the cubed bread. Stir in vinegar just before serving.

If you use an electric blender, mix garlic, pepper, salt, cumin seed, coarsely chopped tomatoes, olive oil, and ½ cup water simultaneously for a few seconds on low speed. Proceed as directed above.

AJO BLANCO CON UVAS
(*MALAGAN GAZPACHO*)

SERVINGS: 4 to 5

1¼ cups raw, scalded almonds
white part of 4 slices of bread, soaked in wine vinegar and squeezed

2 medium cloves garlic, peeled
4 cups ice water
⅔ cup olive oil
7–8 peeled white grapes per serving

Using a mortar, pound almonds with garlic and bread, gradually add olive oil, strain, and stir in ice water. Serve very cold with seven or eight peeled white grapes in each soup plate.

If you use an electric blender, mix all ingredients except grapes simultaneously until almonds are ground as fine as possible; strain and serve as described above.

GAZPACHO EXTREMEÑO
(*ESTREMADURAN GAZPACHO*)

SERVINGS: 4

2 medium cloves garlic, peeled
1 medium green pepper, seeded and cut in strips
salt to taste

white part of 3 slices of bread
1 large or 2 small eggs
6 TB olive oil
4 tsp wine vinegar
4 cups ice water

If you use a mortar, crush garlic with pepper and a little salt. Add bread previously soaked in water and squeezed. Blend in lightly beaten eggs. Gradually add olive oil while stirring. Strain into deep bowl, stir in ice water, add vinegar, check seasoning, and serve very cold.

In an electric blender, you can mix all the ingredients except the ice water simultaneously. Blend on low speed for only a few seconds, then strain and proceed as described above.

GAZPACHUELO

SERVINGS: 4

*1½–2-lb. fish, cleaned
and cut in slices ***
juice of 1 lemon
2 egg yolks

3 small potatoes, peeled
⅓ cup olive oil
6 cups water
salt and pepper to taste

Bring water to a boil with salt. Boil fish, covered, for 20 minutes with peeled potatoes cut in half. Remove potatoes when cooked through. Strain soup and return it to low fire.

Put egg yolks in a mortar with a few drops of lemon juice. Blend. Little by little add olive oil at room temperature while stirring constantly in the same direction. When the sauce is very thick, add 2 TB lemon juice. Gradually stir in remaining olive oil. Season with salt and pepper.

Slide the egg whites into the soup. When they are cooked, remove with skimmer or slotted spoon, drain, and dice. Dice the cooked potatoes. Cool to lukewarm ½ cup of the soup and gradually add it to the mayonnaise while stirring. Stir in the remaining lemon juice. Gradually blend in the rest of the soup. Remove bones and skin from fish, return fish to soup, add the diced potatoes and egg whites, reheat gently, and serve.

NOTE: In Málaga, the gazpachuelo is eaten lukewarm.

* Use any lean white fish, small or large, cleaned, but with heads and tails. The greater the variety, the better.

CHAPTER 5

SOUPS

SOUP plays an important role in Spanish meals. Light soups are always included in informal dinners, and substantial soups often constitute the entire family supper. Among the hearty versions are the meat and vegetable soups known as cocidos, for which diverse regional recipes are given at the end of this chapter. There are a few vegetable broths, but outside of the cocidos, the most popular are garlic or fish soups.

FISH SOUPS

Every coastal province has a fish soup, many of them delicious brews on the order of the bouillabaisse. The kinds of fish used and the seasonings vary from region to region. Some provinces like saffron, tomato, and onion; others like garlic and lemon. Some put in ham or egg, and one recipe from the Cádiz coast calls for orange juice.

Many fish soups are thickened with bread; others include potatoes to make a meal in one dish. The following recipes are from distinct regions; the first is particularly popular in Madrid, which, although it has no coast, has its choice of fresh fish from all of Spain.

SOPA AL CUARTO DE HORA
(QUARTER-OF-AN-HOUR SOUP)

SERVINGS: 6

2 TB *olive oil*	*½ lb. clams in the shell*
½ lb. shrimp	*1 hard-boiled egg*
2 oz. *cured ham, diced*	2 TB *raw rice*
¼ cup shelled peas, fresh or frozen	*½ tsp paprika*
	½ tsp salt
2 small tomatoes	*a pinch of black pepper*
1 small onion, chopped fine	*4½ cups boiling water*

Rinse clams in cold water and let sit in bowl of water for at least an hour to remove sand. Cook clams until they open in water to cover. Remove one shell from each, set aside, and pass the liquid through a kitchen towel or cloth in order to strain out any remaining sand. Shell the peas and the uncooked shrimp. Scald the rice by throwing it in boiling water for 3 minutes, then straining and rinsing it under cold water.

Heat olive oil in a skillet and brown the ham. Put ham aside and slowly fry the finely chopped onion in the same oil. When the onion is golden, add the tomatoes forced through a sieve. Let the tomatoes and onions fry together for 5 minutes before adding the paprika with the pan off the fire. Immediately pour in 4½ cups of boiling water. Add the peeled shrimp and peas and the scalded rice, ½ tsp salt, and a pinch of black pepper. Let the soup boil for exactly 15 minutes. (This is the quarter of an hour to which the soup owes its name.) Just before serving, add the clams, the liquid in which they cooked, the ham, and the hard-boiled egg, chopped fine. Check seasoning and serve.

SOPA DE PESCADO A LA VASCA
(BASQUE FISH SOUP)

The quality of fish soup depends on the quality of the fish. The following way of preparing it is Basque, but the kind of fish used can be varied according to what is locally available. You might use a head of hake, some crabs, and a few crayfish. Or you might use, as suggested below, mussels, rockfish, and sea bass. All fish and shellfish must be cleaned, but the heads, bones, and shellfish carcasses (all of which are strained out afterward) are cooked in the soup to give it flavor.

SERVINGS: 6

3 doz. mussels
3–4 lbs. small whole fish, cleaned and cut into several pieces. Any white fish can be used: rockfish and small sea bass, for example
4 medium cloves garlic, minced
3 medium carrots, diced
1 medium onion, minced

2 leeks or 4–5 small shallots, minced (omit if not available)
6 TB olive oil
¼ cup cognac
center of 3 slices of white bread
a sprig of thyme
1 bay leaf
10 cups water
salt and pepper to taste
1 rounded TB butter

Fry garlic, carrots, onion, and leeks or shallots in olive oil very slowly for 15 minutes. Add a sprig of thyme and a bay leaf. Put in fish and fry gently for 3 minutes. Heat cognac, pour it over fish and vegetables, light it, and let flames die. Pour in 10 cups water, let it come to a boil over a fairly high flame and boil slowly for 15 minutes. While it boils, open the mussels in a saucepan over moderate heat with a little water. Strain the juice through a kitchen towel and add it to the fish and vegetables. Remove mussels from shell and set aside. Cut or tear the white part of three slices of bread into small bits. Strain the soup into another saucepan, add the bits of bread, and cook it in the soup 10 minutes more. Separate all the fish meat from the bones. Strain the soup a second time, forcing undissolved bits of bread through strainer. Season with salt and pepper. Simmer fish meat and shelled mussels in the soup for 5 minutes before serving; add butter just before removing from fire, stir to mix, and serve very hot.

SOPA DE PESCADO A LA CATALANA
(*CATALAN FISH SOUP*)

SERVINGS: 6

*3–4 lbs. fish, cleaned
and cut in slices, and
shellfish, cleaned ***

1 small onion, minced

*1 medium tomato,
chopped*

⅓ cup olive oil

3 cloves garlic, peeled

*12 peeled, toasted
almonds*

10 cups water

*4 slices white bread cut
in fine shavings*

1 bay leaf

2 sprigs parsley

salt and pepper to taste

* Use any lean white fish, small or large, cleaned, but with heads and tails. Any shellfish is suitable: for example, a few clams or mussels and four or five shrimp or small crabs or a crayfish.

Put fish in 10 cups boiling salt water. Boil 15 minutes covered. Heat olive oil. Fry minced onion. When it takes on color, add tomato. Let tomato liquid reduce. Add tomato-onion mixture, bay leaf, and parsley to fish when it has been boiling 15 minutes. Boil 15 minutes longer, covered. Place bread shavings in a separate pot. Strain fish soup over bread and return soup to fire. Crush almonds with garlic in a mortar; add to soup. Boil soup slowly 10 minutes more while separating shells, bones, and skin from fish and shellfish. Strain soup a second time, reheat with cleaned fish and shellfish, season, and serve.

SOPA DE PESCADO GADITANA
(FISH SOUP OF CÁDIZ)

2½–3 lbs. large and small fish, cleaned and cut in slices 2–3" thick *

4 small garlic cloves, peeled

1 medium onion, minced

½ cup sour orange juice (add lemon juice if oranges are sweet)

10 cups boiling water

salt and pepper to taste

Salt fish lightly and let it stand for 1 hour. Heat olive oil and fry whole garlic cloves until browned. Remove garlic. Fry minced onion for 1 minute; pour in 10 cups boiling water. Boil until onion is soft. Add fish slices, cover, and boil 15–20 minutes longer. Strain soup and return to low fire. Remove bones and skin from fish. Stir in orange juice, season to taste, return fish to soup, reheat, and serve.

* Use any lean white fish, small or large, cleaned, but with heads and tails. The greater the variety, the better.

CREMA DE CARRAMARES A LA DONOSTIARRA
(*CRAB BISQUE*)

The creation of Señor Candido Tojal Varela, chef of the Hotel San Sebastián in San Sebastián, this soup won a prize in the First Gastronomic Competition of the Province of Guipuzcoa.

SERVINGS: 12 generous helpings

3–4 *doz. very small, live crabs, well washed and rinsed in several changes of water*	1 *cup butter*
	½ *cup olive oil*
	⅔ *cup cognac*
	⅔ *cup dry white wine*
4 *doz. tiny shrimp, peeled and cleaned*	1½ *cups cream*
	4 *egg yolks*
3 *small shallots, diced*	17 *cups water*
1 *medium onion, sliced thin*	¾ *cup rice flour diluted in 2 cups water*
3 *small carrots, diced*	*a few sprigs of parsley*
white part of 1 medium leek, diced	*a sprig of fresh tarragon*
1 *medium tomato, peeled, seeded, and chopped*	½ *tsp cayenne pepper*
	salt to taste

Heat ½ cup butter with ½ cup olive oil in a large saucepan. Add shallots. When they take on color, add onion, carrots, and leeks. Brown vegetables lightly over moderate fire, then simmer very slowly for 30 minutes, taking care not to let the butter burn. After 15 minutes, add parsley and tarragon. After a total of 30 minutes, add the peeled, seeded, and chopped tomato and let it reduce to a pulp.

70

Put the live crabs in a deep receptacle. Mash them to a pulp with the end of a heavy chopping board. Increase heat under vegetables. Add crab pulp. Warm ⅔ cup cognac in a separate saucepan and light it. Pour flaming cognac over crabs; let flame die down while stirring. Mix in cayenne pepper and dry white wine. Cook mixture 5 minutes with an occasional stir. Pour over it 17 cups of water. When the water is hot, add rice flour diluted in 2 cups of water. Salt to taste. Stir and let soup cook slowly 30–35 minutes. Remove foam from soup as it forms.

Before serving, slice peeled shrimp and fry in remaining butter over moderate fire. Do not let butter brown. Strain soup. Beat yolks of three eggs in a large bowl. In another bowl, put 1½ cups of cream. Blend a cup or two of strained soup with the cream, then add the mixture gradually to the egg yolks while stirring. Return the resulting mixture to the pot of soup while stirring over a low fire. Heat if necessary, but in no case allow to come to a boil. Serve in shallow bowls topped with fried shrimp.

SOPA DE AJO (GARLIC SOUP)

Garlic soup is one of the most characteristic foods of Spain and constitutes one of Spain's two contributions to soupmaking, according to an authority on Spanish food.* In its simplest form composed of garlic, bread, olive oil, and water, garlic soup has little appeal outside the Spanish hearth. In its more luxurious versions it is a very good soup, well worth serving, and considered by Spaniards the

* Marquesa de Parabere, author of *Historia de la Gastronomía,* Madrid: Espasa-Calpe, S.A., 1943. The other contribution is the cocido, or *olla,* which the French made into pot-au-feu.

best possible protection and cure for the effects of overeating. Ways of preparing it vary not only from region to region but from individual to individual. Some like it liquid; some dry. Some like the bread soaked and dissolved; some like it crisp. The Basques make it with tomato and omit paprika; the Madrileños always put in paprika. In Navarre, it is made with stock from a calf's foot; the Malagueñans prefer it with fish stock. The traditional way to serve it is in an earthenware bowl.

SOPA DE AJO AL PESCADO
(*GARLIC SOUP WITH FISH STOCK*)

SERVINGS: 4

6 *paper-thin slices of whole-wheat bread*	4½ *cups white fish stock*
2 *cloves of garlic*	1 *tsp paprika*
5 TB *olive oil*	*salt to taste*

Heat fish stock in a pan. In a skillet or earthenware casserole, fry garlic cloves slowly in heated olive oil; when they are browned, discard them. Fry the bread slices until browned, adding oil if necessary. Remove pan from fire to stir in the paprika; pour on boiling fish stock and return to fire. Break up the bread with a spoon when it softens. Salt to taste. Cover and cook over low fire 15–20 minutes. Serve in large soup bowls.

NOTE: This soup is even better if you have bits of white fish and slices of shellfish from the fish stock or from a previously made fish dish. If you have a quantity of fish to add, omit two of the bread slices. Add the cooked fish and shellfish during the last 5 minutes so that they have time to heat through, but do not cook long enough to fall apart.

SOPA DE AJO AL HUEVO
(GARLIC SOUP WITH EGG)

SERVINGS: 4

6 *paper-thin slices of whole-wheat bread*

2 *cloves of garlic*

5 TB *olive oil*

1 *tsp paprika*

4½ *cups meat or chicken stock (or canned beef or chicken bouillon)*

2 *eggs*

salt and pepper to taste

This soup is best made in a flat earthenware casserole about 8 inches in diameter, but you can make it in any dish that has a fairly large frying surface and can be put in the oven.

Preheat oven to 450°. Heat olive oil until it smokes, let it cool slightly, and fry the whole garlic cloves gently. Discard when browned. Fry the bread until browned, remove casserole from fire to stir in paprika, pour in preheated bouillon or stock, and return to fire. Break up bread when soft, season to taste with salt and pepper, and cook slowly, covered, 15–20 minutes.

A few minutes before serving, beat eggs with a little salt, spread them over the surface of the soup, and put the uncovered dish in the oven until a brown crust forms on top.

NOTE: For a variation, instead of making the oven crust, poach one egg per person in the soup. (It is easiest to avoid breaking the yolk if you break the egg into a saucer and slide it from the saucer into the soup.) You can also beat two eggs with a little salt and stir them into the soup. This is the way preferred in Madrid.

COCIDO (MEAT AND VEGETABLE SOUP)

Every country has a way of preparing a hearty soup of vegetables and meat simmered in water for a long time and eaten all in one dish or in two courses: the soup, followed by the meat and vegetables. France has its pot-au-feu or *petite marmite,* Russia its borscht, and so on. In Spain, there is a soup of this type in every region, each making use of the ingredients easily available locally.

One thing all these soups have in common in Spain is the use of ham, bacon, pork, or pork sausages. L. A. de Vega traces the origin of the dish to the late fifteenth century when the converted Jews, in order to convince their neighbors that they had been truly converted, began substituting pork for cooked eggs in a traditional Jewish dish known in Spain as Adafina.*

In the popular or peasant versions, everything is served in the soup bowl. There are many dried vegetables, but little meat—perhaps only a piece of smoked ham to give flavor. In the more bourgeois cocidos, the broth is usually strained and served as a first course with rice or very small noodles boiled in it. For the second course, the meat is heaped in slices on a platter surrounded by the vegetables. Sometimes there are two platters, one for the vegetables, the more fragile sausages, and the bacon; the other for the meat, chicken, and ham. The dish is most often called a cocido (*cocido* means "boiled"), but in some regions, it is named after the pot in which it is cooked: the *pote* of the Asturias, the *puchero* of La Mancha, the *olla* of Santander and Catalonia. In Galicia, it is referred to as a *caldo,* a

* *Gastronomía España,* published by the Ministerio de Información y Turismo.

74

comprehensive term meaning broth, stock, sauce, wine, and alcohol.

Let us start with a Caldo Gallego. The following is a peasant version as described to me by the owner of the excellent Galician restaurant Oscar in Madrid—a far-from-peasant restaurant.

CALDO GALLEGO I

SERVINGS: 4 large bowls

¾ *cup dried white beans*

¼ *lb. smoked ham*

¼ *lb. lean smoked bacon or salt pork (1 thick slice)*

7 *cups water*

½ *medium onion, sliced*

½ *small head white cabbage*

3 *turnips*

a few turnip greens

salt and pepper to taste

Pour 7 cups cold water over the beans, ham, and bacon in an earthenware pot. Cover and just barely simmer for 2½ hours. Add the sliced onion and the cabbage, turnips, and turnip tops, all chopped in fairly large pieces. Mix, but stir as little as possible in order not to bruise the beans. Salt and pepper to taste and simmer 1½ hours more. Serve in large soup bowls with meat cut in bite-size pieces.

NOTE: In Galicia, the base of all *caldos* is *unto,* an aged bacon sometimes three, four, or five years old. The smoked ham and bacon or salt pork are suggested as American substitutes and are used as substitutes in Spain outside Galicia.

CALDO GALLEGO II

This is a bourgeois version of the *caldo* and makes a hearty two-course meal. It is sometimes referred to as a

"Pote" Gallego to distinguish it from the humbler *caldo,* but I have it on authority that *pote* is a Madrid term; Galicians refer to either version as Caldo Gallego.

SERVINGS: 6 to 8

½ *lb. smoked ham*
½ *lb. cured, unsmoked ham*
1 lb. veal
¼ *lb. smoked bacon (in 1 slice) or ¼ lb. salt pork*
1 pork sausage
¼ *stewing chicken (optional)*
1 cup dried white beans

½ *medium head white cabbage, chopped coarsely*
4 turnips cut in two
a few tender turnip greens
1 lb. potatoes cut in quarters
½ *medium onion, sliced*
½ *chorizo (or pepperoni) sausage*
salt and pepper to taste

Put the ham, veal, bacon, pork sausage, and stewing chicken in an earthenware pot, cover with cold water, put on lid, season, and simmer as slowly as possible for 4 hours. An hour after putting on the meat, place the white beans in a second pot, pour in cold water to the level of the beans, and add 4 more cups of water. Simmer the beans slowly until almost tender, then add the cabbage, turnips, turnip tops, potatoes, onion, and the whole *chorizo* (or pepperoni) sausage. Continue simmering slowly, adding boiling water if necessary to keep food covered. When the vegetables are almost cooked, combine the vegetables and their broth with the meat, season to taste, and let it all simmer together another half hour. Serve the liquid first as a soup, followed by the meat, pork sausage, bacon, and chicken cut into serving pieces on one platter, accompanied by the vegetables on a second platter with the *chorizo*.

While the Caldo Gallego uses white beans, chick-peas are the foundation of the cocidos of central Spain. Even there, each region has its variations. The Cocido Andaluz uses beef, pork, sausages, squash, green beans, and a seasoning of garlic, saffron, and pepper crushed together in a mortar. The Olla of Córdoba has only chick-peas, bacon, and cabbage, cooked just enough to be tender. The Cocido Madrileño is a hearty dish, suited to the cold, dry winters of Madrid.

COCIDO MADRILEÑO

SERVINGS: 4–5

½ lb. chick-peas, pre-soaked in water at least 10 hrs.

11 cups water

½ lb. veal or beef

3–4 oz. ham

5 oz. bacon or salt pork in 1 slice

4 medium potatoes, cut in two

1 3–4-oz. pork sausage

½ small head cabbage, chopped coarsely

¼ stewing chicken (optional)

1 marrow bone

3 carrots

1 leek (if not available, substitute a small onion)

a sprig of mint

⅓ cup raw rice or ½ cup fine noodles

salt to taste

3 TB olive oil

1 garlic clove

Bring 11 cups of water to boil in a large pot. When it boils, add the presoaked chick-peas, drained and tied in cheesecloth. Add veal, ham, bacon, chicken, marrow bone, carrots, leek, and mint. When soup boils again, skim it well and cook on low flame for 2 hours. Add potatoes and salt to taste. Cook approximately 1 hour longer.

In the meantime, prick the pork sausage with a needle so that it will not burst, and put it in a separate pot with the cabbage and water to cover. Bring to a boil and simmer.

A half hour before serving, stir the pot containing the meat, ham, chicken, etc., and strain out 6 cups of broth. Heat it to boiling, put in the raw rice or noodles, and cook until tender.

When the cabbage and pork sausage are cooked, drain well and fry in 3 TB olive oil in which a garlic clove has been previously browned and removed.

Serve the broth containing rice or noodles as the first course. For the second course, put the chick-peas, well drained, in the center of an oval serving dish with the potatoes at either end and slices of carrot along the sides. Slice the meat, ham, bacon, and chicken and put it on top of the chick-peas. Serve the cabbage in a vegetable dish with the pork sausage chopped fine on top. On the side, serve a thick tomato sauce (p. 193) or a parsley sauce (p. 194).

PELOTA
(MEAT DUMPLING)

While not indispensable, the *pelota* is an agreeable addition to Cocido Madrileño.

3 oz. veal or beef	2 TB olive oil for frying
2–3 small pieces ham	dry bread crumbs
2 slices smoked bacon	a pinch of nutmeg (op-
1 egg	tional)
a pinch of ground clove (optional)	

Put the meat, ham, and bacon through the meat grinder. Add 1 raw egg and enough bread crumbs to make it possible to form a compact ball. Season the mixture with salt, pepper, nutmeg, and ground clove. Make an elongated dumpling, roll it in flour or more bread crumbs, fry it in hot olive oil, and put it in the pot with the meat to cook a half hour before serving. The finer the meat is ground and the more the mixture is worked after the addition of bread crumbs and egg, the finer the dumpling will be.

NOTE: A little minced garlic and parsley may be substituted for nutmeg and ground clove if you like.

In addition to chicken, ham, and sausage, the Catalan version of cocido has a bit of every starch: white beans, chick-peas, noodles, rice, potatoes—an unexpected combination, but surprisingly delicious.

ESCUDELLA DE PAGÉS
(CATALAN PEASANT SOUP)
SERVINGS: 4

½ cup dry white beans
1 small ham bone
1 marrow bone (veal or beef)
¼ chicken or 2 small serving pieces
6 thick slices cooked pork sausage
2 thin slices cured ham (the size of the palm of your hand)

8 cups cold water
½ head cabbage cut in chunks
1 large potato cut in eighths
¼ cup raw rice
1 cup thin noodles
1 cup cooked chick-peas
1 tsp salt
pepper to taste

79

Rinse the beans in cold water and tie the bones in cheesecloth. Put both with the chicken, sausage, and ham in a pot or casserole with 8 cups of cold water and salt. Bring to a boil, reduce flame, and cook gently, covered, about 2 hours or until beans are cooked and chicken very tender. Remove ham and marrow bones and discard them. Put chicken aside. If there is little liquid left, add a bit of water for the cooking of the remaining ingredients and bring soup to a rapid boil. When it is boiling, put in the cabbage, potatoes, rice, noodles, chick-peas, and pepper. Continue cooking over medium flame for 30 minutes (or until newly added ingredients are cooked through). A few minutes before serving, put the chicken meat, removed from bones and shredded, in the pot to heat. Correct seasoning and serve.

NOTE: Unlike many stews and soups, this one is only good the day it is made, and is best served immediately. It should be very thick: it is as much stew as soup and constitutes a hearty one-dish meal.

CHAPTER 6

TORTILLAS AND OTHER EGG DISHES

A TORTILLA is a dry cornmeal pancake in Mexico; in Spain, it is an omelet. Spanish tortillas are of two basic kinds: "French," or rolled, and "Spanish," or round. The Gallic origin of the "French" omelet is open to doubt and dispute. Some Spanish authorities claim the French discovered it when it was presented to the court of Louis XIV by the queen's Spanish cook under the name "Tortilla a la Cartuja" (Carthusian Omelet). Others believe it was probably invented in a French monastery before the Carthusian Order spread to Spain.

Whatever the omelet's ancestry, the most suitable pan to cook it in is a heavy, black, cast-iron skillet 7–9 inches in diameter, and all cookbooks will recommend that you devote it to omelet making exclusively. In most kitchens, this is not practical. What is most important about the pan you use for omelets is that it is *never washed:* after use, wipe it clean with a paper towel, then oil it if necessary. Secondly, you should avoid cooking in it any recipe calling for acid ingredients (tomatoes, lemon juice, vinegar, wine), particularly in quantity. If you observe these two rules, food will not stick in the pan unless allowed to burn. If food burns, try to clean the pan with salt or with a dry brush and cooking oil. If that does not work and you are forced to resort to soap and water, heat oil in the pan afterward, pour off the oil, dry the pan with a paper towel, and wipe it with fresh oil. By repeating this after every use for a few days, you will restore the surface.

In Spain, omelets are served as a separate course or an accompaniment to a first course. One large omelet might be put on the table to be divided into quarters by four people and eaten along with salad and a bit of sausage. Several omelets, each with a distinct filling, can be presented piled on top each other (for example, a potato omelet, an onion omelet, a white bean omelet, and an eggplant omelet), the layers held together by a thick tomato sauce.

BASIC INSTRUCTIONS FOR "SPANISH" OR ROUND OMELET

Fry all the ingredients except the eggs in hot olive oil (usually about ¼ cup). When cooked, allow ingredients to cool at least 5 minutes before adding them to a bowl containing the eggs lightly beaten with salt. Stir mixture while reheating frying pan with additional oil (if needed to cover the bottom of the pan). When oil is on the verge of smoking, pour in mixture and keep shaking pan and sliding a spatula or knife around the edges of the omelet to keep it free and to form a high, rounded edge. When the omelet is almost firm, hold a plate upside down against the frying pan; invert both, dropping the omelet onto the plate as you do so, then slip the omelet back into the pan browned side up. This is easiest to do if the plate you use fits neatly inside the frying pan. Shake pan while the second side browns. Serve at once.

CATALAN ONION OMELET

SERVINGS: 2

> *1 large onion, chopped*   *4 eggs*
> *3* TB *olive oil*   *salt to taste*

Heat olive oil to verge of smoking and fry chopped onion rapidly until well browned; stir frequently. Beat 2 eggs in each of two bowls with salt. When onions have browned and cooled slightly, divide them and put half in each bowl. Stir mixture and make two omelets following instructions for "Spanish" Omelet (above).

ANDALUSIAN ONION OMELET

Catalan Onion Omelet is a good, rapidly made dish. Andalusian Onion Omelet is a kind of miracle; it is more than the sum of its parts. The long, slow frying of huge quantities of onion reduces them to a purée which blends with the eggs to produce an extraordinary dish, well worth the time it takes.

SERVINGS: 2 generous helpings

7 *cups of very finely chopped onions (4–5 large onions)*	¼ *cup olive oil* 4 *eggs* *salt to taste*

Heat ¼ cup olive oil until it crinkles, but is not yet smoking. Put the finely chopped onion to fry over a hot flame. Cover and do not stir during the first 20 minutes. Thereafter it will be necessary to stir the onions more and more frequently to prevent sticking. When the onions have been reduced to a soft, brown purée (after about an hour's cooking), put them aside for at least 5 minutes. (This much may be done several hours in advance if more convenient.)

Divide the onion mixture in two and add half to each of two bowls containing two eggs beaten with a generous amount of salt. Stir the mixture. Reheat the frying pan. You should not have to add oil for the first omelet, but may need to for the second. Pour in the onion-egg mixture when the oil in the frying pan begins to smoke, and continue as in the basic "Spanish" Omelet (p. 82).

ANDALUSIAN ONION AND POTATO OMELET

SERVINGS: 2–4

1 *big onion* 5 *small potatoes*	½ *cup olive oil* 4 *eggs*
salt and pepper to taste	

Cut potatoes lengthwise in fine slices. Heat ½ cup olive oil in large frying pan. Fry potatoes lightly while chopping onion. Push potatoes into a corner of pan, add chopped onion, and put potatoes on top of onion. Season with salt and pepper. While they cook, chop the potatoes and onion with a spoon or spatula until they are almost a purée. (The potatoes and onion can be fried several hours in advance with equally good results.)

Allow potato-onion mixture to cool at least 5 minutes before dividing in equal parts and adding to 2 bowls, each containing 2 eggs beaten with salt. Continue as instructed in basic "Spanish" Omelet (p. 82).

The onion and potato omelet may be served hot or cold as a first course or part of a cold supper.

TORTILLA DE PATATA A LA ESPAÑOLA
(*SPANISH POTATO OMELET* [*from Castile*])

SERVINGS: 1

1 medium potato   *2 eggs*
1 small onion   *¼ cup olive oil*
1 slice cured ham   *salt to taste*
   (1 oz.)

Cut potato in thin slices. Chop onion fine. Cut ham into small pieces. Heat olive oil to verge of smoking and fry ham. When it is slightly browned, add onions. When onions are soft and golden, add potatoes. After potatoes are cooked, allow mixture to cool a few minutes before adding to two eggs beaten with a pinch of salt. Proceed as in instructions for basic "Spanish" Omelet (p. 82).

WHITE BEAN OMELET

SERVINGS: 1

¾ cup dried white   *2 eggs*
   beans, cooked (p.   *¼ cup olive oil*
   185)   *a large pinch of salt*

85

Heat olive oil in skillet; fry beans lightly and remove. Allow them to cool a few minutes before adding to bowl containing eggs beaten with salt. Continue as in basic instructions for "Spanish" Omelet (p. 82).

ASPARAGUS OMELET

SERVINGS: 1

4 asparagus tips, cooked
   (or canned or
   frozen)

2 eggs
1/4 cup olive oil
a pinch of salt

Boil fresh asparagus 15–20 minutes or until tender. Only the tender parts of fresh asparagus should be used in the omelet. Cut into 1-inch pieces, heat briefly in hot olive oil, and allow to cool a few minutes before adding to bowl containing two eggs beaten with salt. Proceed as in instructions for basic "Spanish" Omelet (p. 82).

CHICK-PEA OMELET

SERVINGS: 1

1 thick slice bacon
1 small slice ham
a few slices cooked pork
   sausage
1/2 TB olive oil

1/2 cup canned or cooked
   chick-peas (see p.
   184 for cooking in-
   structions)
salt and pepper to taste

2 eggs

Cut bacon in squares and fry it in the olive oil. When bacon is browned, add ham cut fine, pork sausage sliced, and chick-peas, drained. Sprinkle with black pepper and salt. Fry until chick-peas begin to brown. Cool slightly before adding to bowl containing two beaten eggs. Proceed as in instructions for basic "Spanish" Omelet (p. 82).

EGGPLANT OMELET

SERVINGS: 1

½ eggplant   ¼ cup olive oil
2 eggs   a pinch of salt

Cut eggplant in half lengthwise and slice crosswise. Salt it and allow to stand a half hour. Squeeze out liquid and fry in hot oil. When browned, allow to cool, add to bowl containing two beaten eggs, and proceed as in instructions for basic "Spanish" Omelet (p. 82).

BASIC INSTRUCTIONS FOR "FRENCH" OR ROLLED OMELET

Cover the bottom of the frying pan with olive oil (about 1½ TB for a pan 7 inches in diameter). Heat oil over a brisk fire until it is on the verge of smoking. Brown the ingredients and remove them to a plate. If necessary to cover the surface of the pan, add more olive oil. Pour in eggs beaten with salt. Stir them quickly with a fork as if you intended to scramble them. Cover the center third with the ingredients of the omelet, fold the two sides over the center, one by one, and slide the omelet upside down onto a plate, ready to serve. The omelet should be browned on the outside; slightly runny inside.

87

MUSHROOM OMELET

SERVINGS: 1

½ cup mushrooms	2 TB olive oil
1–2 TB chopped parsley	2 eggs
	salt and pepper to taste

Fry mushrooms over medium heat in enough olive oil to cover bottom of pan. When mushrooms are soft and turning brown, add chopped parsley. Season with salt and pepper. Stir and remove to plate. Add olive oil to cover the surface of the pan if necessary, pour in eggs lightly beaten, and proceed as in instructions for "French" Omelet (p. 87).

TORTILLA A LA PAISANA
(OMELET WITH HAM AND VEGETABLES)

SERVINGS: 1

2 TB cooked green beans, cut in 1" lengths	2 TB diced, cooked potatoes
1 TB green peas, cooked or canned	½ tsp tomato paste
1 TB ham cut in bits	2 TB olive oil
	2 eggs lightly beaten
	a pinch of salt

Put enough olive oil in the frying pan to cover the bottom (about 1½ TB). Heat the oil over a brisk fire until it is on the verge of smoking. Throw in green beans and potatoes; stir with a fork for a few seconds, then add ham. When the mixture is lightly browned, add peas and tomato paste. Mix. Remove to a plate. Add olive oil if necessary to cover the bottom of the pan and heat it to the

88

verge of smoking before pouring in two eggs beaten with a pinch of salt. Stir eggs quickly with a fork. Cover the center third with the vegetables and ham and proceed as in instructions for basic "French" Omelet (p. 87).

HUEVOS AL NIDO (I)
(*EGGS IN A NEST*)

SERVINGS: 6

6 *fairly small, soft rolls (about 3" in diameter)*	6 TB *milk*
	½ *cup olive oil for frying*
6 *egg yolks*	2 TB *pine nuts (optional)*
5 *eggs whites*	
3 TB *butter*	*salt*

Cut the tops off the rolls leaving a little over half. You will use only the bottom half. Scoop out most of the soft white interior; take care not to pierce the sides. Pour 1 TB milk in each roll, divide the butter among the six, and put an egg yolk in each. Sprinkle the yolks lightly with salt.

Heat olive oil until hot (but not smoking) while you beat the egg whites to a stiff peak. Dividing them equally among the six rolls, pile the whites on top the yolks and sprinkle with pine nuts. Fry the rolls in the hot oil, spooning oil over the whites until they puff up and are lightly browned. Serve at once: the whites fall fairly quickly (although they stay stiff as long as a well-cooked soufflé).

NOTE: An inexpensive and effective first course, this recipe must be made at the last moment. If the raw egg whites are voluminous when beaten, do not use all of them.

HUEVOS AL NIDO (II)
(*EGGS IN A NEST*)

SERVINGS: 6

6 *fairly small, soft rolls* | 3 TB *butter*
(*about 3" in diame-* | 6 *eggs*
ter) | ½ *cup olive oil*
12 TB *milk* | *a pinch of salt*

Cut a hole in the top of each roll and remove a plug. Hollow out the inside of the buns with care not to pierce the sides. Put 2 TB milk in each roll, divide the butter among the six, and put an egg yolk in each. Sprinkle yolks with salt and cover them with the whites, beaten just enough to blend. Replace the plug and fry the rolls in enough hot oil to cover the pan liberally. While frying, spoon the oil over the bread to heat it through and brown the crust evenly. Serve hot.

HUEVOS AL PLATO A LA FLAMENCA
(*BAKED EGGS WITH HAM AND SAUSAGE*)

SERVINGS: 4

8 *eggs*
8 *small slices of*
chorizo (*or pep-*
peroni) *sausage*
4 oz. *cured ham*
½ *sweet red pepper,*
canned or precooked
2 *small tomatoes,*
peeled and chopped
½ *cup plus* 2 TB *olive*
oil

2 *heaping* TB *peas,*
cooked or canned
2 *heaping* TB *green*
beans, cooked or
canned
2 TB *asparagus tips,*
cooked or canned
a few drops of sherry
a few drops of bouillon
a pinch of salt

Cut half the ham into small cubes; divide remainder into eight triangular pieces. Cut pepper into eight similar triangles. Peel and seed tomatoes and chop them. Dice green beans and asparagus tips. Preheat oven to 375°.

Heat ½ cup olive oil and fry the cubed ham. When it is browned, add the potatoes, peas, beans, and asparagus tips. When they are caught, add the tomatoes and sprinkle over the mixture a few drops of sherry and a few drops of bouillon. Let it cook for a few minutes until the sauce is reduced.

The eggs can be made in one large flat baking dish or in individual ramekins (of porcelain, pyrex, or earthenware). Line the dish or dishes with the contents of the frying pan and add the eggs one by one, breaking them first into a saucer, then sliding them into the baking dish. Fry the slices of *chorizo* and the triangles of ham lightly in the remaining olive oil. Sprinkle a little salt on the whites of the eggs only. Decorate the edges of the dish or dishes with alternating pieces of *chorizo,* ham, and pepper. Sprinkle the oil from the frying of the *chorizo* and ham over the top, place the dish in a pan of boiling water and bake in a preheated 375° oven for 6–10 minutes or until the whites are cooked but the yolks still tremble slightly. Serve at once.

NOTE: This is an unabbreviated version of the renowned classic dish from Seville, the recipe of a chef and gastronomic authority. It makes an economical and very decorative first course.

CHAPTER 7

PAELLA AND
OTHER RICE DISHES

PAELLA is beyond doubt the Spanish dish best known beyond Spain's frontiers. Usually only one dish on a menu or in a recipe book is called a paella: the Paella Valenciana. However, the contents of the dish so labeled are hardly ever the same twice. The word *paella* refers to the special metal pan traditionally used for making rice dishes in the area of Valencia, halfway down Spain's Mediterranean coast. Most of the dishes made in the paella go under the title of rices: Arroz a la Alicantina (Alicante Rice), Arroz con Pollo (Rice with Chicken), etc.

The question: "What goes into the true Paella Valenciana?" seldom brings two answers alike in Spain except, perhaps, for the general statement that it contains a little of everything. Spanish gastronomic authorities disagree with this; some speak with disdain of the medley that passes for Paella Valenciana almost everywhere. The combination of meat, chicken, shellfish, fish, red peppers, onion, garlic, and various green vegetables with rice has become so generally accepted under that name that even some Valencians have forgotten or choose to overlook the traditional recipe.

The original paella came into being on the shores of the Albufera River near Valencia, where the inhabitants made use of the material at hand. What was at hand was beans, snails, and eels from the river, and, of course, rice, olive oil, and water. These constitute the original paella. Made in the fields, it was eaten by spoonfuls from the dish in which it was cooked and accompanied, not by bread, but by mouthfuls of tender onion.

The traditional Paella Valenciana, another dish altogether, is based on the principle that fish should not be mixed with meat, and that even the combining of various kinds of meats or the mixing of fishes and shellfish of pronounced flavors should be avoided. The first recipe in this section is one for Paella Valenciana as given by no less an authority than the National Rice Cooperative of Valencia, to whom I am indebted for many of these recipes and for valuable hints on the proper cooking of Spanish rices. Those familiar with the Paella Valenciana as it is usually served, both within and outside Spain, will notice that the authentic version does not use onion (as all paellas seem to north of Valencia), nor does it have the red pepper strips which invariably decorate any paella outside its original home. The Valencians feel the pepper negates the flavor of the chicken.

The sumptuous and highly decorative dish that is usually called Paella Valenciana is represented by the recipe for Paella Barcelona Style: it is indeed a mixture of almost everything. Whatever purists from Valencia may feel, it is a very popular dish in Barcelona, where the Catalans are given to mixing flavors (as they do in the Escudella, the Zarzuela, and a number of other Catalan favorites included in this book). A second version of the usual Paella Valenciana follows, less luxurious and less complicated, and thereafter we are on the less disputed ground of the rices, whose variety is infinite.

To make a paella or a rice, you will need a large, round pan with a flat surface and low sides: a frying pan, a fireproof earthenware casserole, or a classic paella pan. The latter is a metal dish with two flattened handles to aid in serving; its sides, gently sloping, are about one and a half inches high. A pan with a diameter of 12–13 inches will serve four to six generously; one with a diameter of 15–16 inches will serve eight or more. Spanish rice is round and short-grained, and use of rice of the same form, whether white or brown, is recommended for all rice dishes given here.

The most important factors in the cooking of Spanish rices are the degree of heat and the length of cooking time after the addition of the rice. Rice is usually added last, after the meat or fish and vegetables have already cooked. The rice is allowed to fry and absorb the sauce for 2–5 minutes. It is stirred while frying and again, briefly, when the water or broth is poured in, but not thereafter. The liquid must be boiling when added, and the flame under the pan must be very high in order to produce an immediate, fast boil. The fire is kept high for 3–5 minutes, or until the rice begins to absorb the liquid and swell. The heat is then reduced so that the rice will continue to absorb the liquid gradually without burning. During the fast boiling of the rice, there is danger of scorching. At the slightest odor of burning, put the bottom of the pan in cold water and return it instantly to a reduced fire. This helps to avoid a burned taste, but it is best and simplest not to have to resort to such measures.

Ideally, the flame should cover the entire bottom surface of the pan. For this reason, all experts agree that the best rices are made outdoors. The pan is put on an iron trident or on three stones of equal height placed in a triangle. A roaring fire whose flames lick the entire surface is kept going throughout the boiling of the rice, then is swiftly pulled apart to leave only embers or glowing sticks for the simmering during which the rice absorbs the remaining liquid and finishes cooking.

Cooking time on low heat should be between 10 and 15 minutes; the nature of the rice and the water, the altitude, and, of course, the amount of heat will vary the cooking time. You can tell when rice is cooked by tasting it and also by looking at it. Study a raw grain of rice. When well cooked it should have the same general outline, although puffed and swollen. When overcooked —something which should never happen—the rice splits open and its profile is completely changed. Overdone rice not only becomes pasty, it loses its flavor. Spanish rice cooks a total of only 15–20 minutes after the liquid is added. Once cooked, it is left in repose off the fire or over the lowest possible heat for 3–4 minutes before being served.

Another element of importance is the amount of liquid, which must be calculated with precision: for most rices, two and a half times the amount of rice (in other words,

2½ cups of water for every cup of rice). The proportions for some rices are 2 to 1. Liquid must be added if the rice is still raw when it has absorbed almost all the juice. Add the minimum necessary and have it boiling hot.

Anyone who follows the basic principles for cooking Spanish rices can master the making of an entire gamut of recipes and turn them out with ease. Rices offer many advantages: they constitute a meal in one dish (at least for the normal American meal), are festive enough for any occasion, as economical or luxurious as you wish, and cause little clutter and confusion in the kitchen at the last minute. Rices are excellent for campfire or backyard cooking, too; that is how they all started.

PAELLA VALENCIANA (I)
(RICE AS MADE IN VALENCIA)

SERVINGS: 4

1 *3-lb. chicken*	*¾ cup peas*
½ cup olive oil	*5 cups boiling water*
1 *small tomato, peeled, seeded, and chopped*	1 TB *paprika*
	a pinch of saffron
1 *medium clove garlic, chopped*	12 *snails, cleaned and ready for cooking*
1 *cup green beans*	2 *cups rice*
salt to taste	

Put 5 cups water to boil. Cut chicken into very small serving pieces, dry pieces with a towel, sprinkle with salt, and fry in very hot olive oil in a medium-sized pan. When chicken has browned for 5 minutes, add the tomato, the garlic, the beans broken into pieces 1–2 inches long, and the peas. Stir while frying for 1 minute. Remove pan from fire to mix in paprika, and on returning it to fire, pour in boiling water. When the mixture boils again, dilute saffron in a little of the boiling liquid and add it with the snails. Salt to taste and let it all cook over a slow fire 15 minutes. Put a little more water to boil on the side.

When the snails and chicken are done, add a little boiling water to make up for what has been lost in the cooking. Bring it to a rapid boil on a hot fire. Add rice. Let it cook rapidly 2–3 minutes, then continue cooking another 10–12 minutes over a low fire. When the rice is done, leave it over the lowest possible heat for another 5 minutes to dry.

PAELLA A LA BARCELONESA
(*RICE BARCELONA STYLE*)

You will need a large pan (about 18 inches in diameter) to hold all the ingredients of this recipe for Barcelona rice, provided by Señorita Maria de Guadalupe Varela.

SERVINGS: 8

½ tender chicken
chicken liver and giblets (optional)
½ lb. squid, cleaned
½ lb. any white fish, cleaned
1 medium onion
2 medium tomatoes
2 garlic cloves
1 green pepper
2 doz. cleaned mussels
½ lb. shrimp

8 cups water
¾ cup olive oil
½ lb. pork spare ribs in small pieces
12 pork sausages (cocktail size)
1 tsp paprika
½ cup peas
a pinch of saffron
3 cups rice
6 canned artichokes
salt to taste

97

OPTIONAL GARNISH:

2 *hard-boiled eggs, sliced*

1 *lobster tail, sliced*

2 *or 3 canned pimientos,*
cut in strips

Cut the chicken into six or more pieces; cut the liver and giblets in half. Cut squid in rings and white fish in small pieces. Mince the onion, peel and chop the tomato, chop the garlic, and slice the green pepper. Put mussels and shrimp in water to cover and cook until mussels open. Remove one shell from each mussel and set mussels and shrimp aside. Put 8 cups of water to boil.

Heat ¾ cup olive oil until it bubbles, then fry the chicken, the spare ribs, and the sausages. Remove them when browned, and in the same oil, fry the onion until golden. Add tomatoes. When the tomato liquid reduces, lower flame and add the paprika, garlic, and green pepper. When these are well mixed and fried, put the chicken, spare ribs, and sausages back in the pan. Stir in the rice. Brown it over a good fire while stirring for about 5 minutes. Add the rings of squid, the boiling water, the peas, the saffron dissolved in a little of the boiling water, and salt to taste. Stir for the last time. Add the cooked shrimp, mussels, and canned artichokes by inserting them in the rice without stirring. Continue cooking at a high temperature until the liquid is absorbed, then let rice simmer until done. Total cooking time should be about 20 minutes.

NOTE: You may omit one or more of the fish, shellfish, meats, and vegetables if you choose. For an even more luxurious paella, garnish it with sliced, cooked lobster, sliced hard-boiled eggs, and canned pimiento cut in strips.

Another, less elaborate version of this kind of paella is the following:

PAELLA VALENCIANA (II)

SERVINGS: 4–6

1 *small chicken*	*½ cup shelled peas*
2 *slices (about 3½ oz.)*	2 *cups rice*
of lean pork	5 *cups boiling water*
⅓ cup olive oil	*a pinch of saffron*
1 *medium tomato,*	8 *crayfish*
peeled, squeezed, and	*½ pound clams, cleaned*
chopped	*and soaked in cold*
2 *garlic cloves, minced*	*water 1 hr. to elimi-*
½ tsp paprika (op-	*nate sand*
tional)	*salt to taste*
½ cup green beans, cut	
in four	

Cut the chicken and the pork into small pieces, season them with salt, and fry in olive oil heated to the verge of smoking in a medium-sized pan. Brown briskly for 5 minutes. Add the tomato, garlic, beans, and peas. When this has browned a little, add the paprika with the pan off the fire. Return pan to fire, put in 2 cups of rice, and fry until rice has browned a little while you bring 5 cups of water to a boil. Add salt to taste, saffron previously crushed in a mortar, and the boiling water. Stir briefly to mix. Cook on high fire for 5 minutes, then on moderate fire another 12–15 minutes. When the rice is half cooked, add crayfish and clams. Once cooked, let rice rest 3–4 minutes before serving.

ARROZ PARELLADA
(RICE WITH BONED CHICKEN AND SHELLED FISH)

SERVINGS: 6

1 small frying chicken cut in a dozen pieces
½ lb. tender roasting pork cut in a dozen pieces
6 crayfish, cleaned
½ lb. squid, cleaned and cut in rounds
2 doz. clams or mussels, cleaned

7 cups water
½ cup olive oil
8 canned artichoke hearts
⅔ cup drained canned or precooked green beans or peas
2 cups rice
a pinch of saffron
salt to taste

Put fish, shellfish, pork, and chicken in a large pot with 7 cups of water. Simmer until chicken and pork are tender. Strain liquid through a sieve. Remove bones from chicken and shells from shellfish.

Heat olive oil in a large pan. Fry chicken and shellfish after patting them dry with a towel. When they are browned, add vegetables and rice; stir until rice is browned. Heat to boiling 5 cups of the liquid in which the fish, pork, and chicken cooked. Pour boiling liquid over rice. Season with salt and a pinch of saffron dissolved in a little of the boiling liquid. Stir just enough to mix. Let it boil hard until the rice begins to absorb the liquid; then reduce flame and continue cooking 10–15 minutes or until rice is done. Let it rest 4–5 minutes before serving.

100

ARROZ MIRAMAR
(A SEAFOOD RICE TYPICAL OF VALENCIA)

SERVINGS: 4

1 doz. mussels, cleaned
4 crayfish or 8 shrimp
5 cups cold water
½ cup olive oil
½ lb. lean pork
¼ lb. cured ham
1 large onion, minced
2 small squid, cut in
   rounds
salt and white pepper to
   taste

1 large slice of any firm
   white fish
2 TB parsley, chopped
1 small clove garlic,
   minced
1 medium tomato,
   peeled and chopped
2 cups rice
8 canned artichoke
   hearts
a pinch of saffron

Preheat oven to 450°. Cover cleaned mussels and crayfish or shrimp with 5 cups cold water and cook until mussels open. Strain and reserve the liquid; discard the mussel shells. Heat olive oil until it is on the verge of smoking. Brown the pork and ham, both cut in small pieces. When they are well fried, add the minced onion, squid, and white fish, boned and cut in pieces. Mix in chopped parsley, garlic, and tomato. Season to taste with salt and white pepper. Add raw rice, cooked mussels and crayfish or shrimp, and canned artichokes. Fry and mix well while you bring to a boil 5 cups of the liquid in which the mussels and shrimp cooked. Dissolve saffron in a little of the boiling liquid. Pour the liquid over the rice, stir in the saffron, correct the seasoning, and boil the rice rapidly for a moment or two; then bake in a hot oven (450°) for about 15 minutes. The rice should absorb all the liquid; the grains should be separate and the surface browned.

ARROZ CON MEJILLONES Y ALMEJAS
(*RICE WITH MUSSELS AND CLAMS*)

SERVINGS: 4

4 lbs. mussels and clams, cleaned	1 medium tomato, peeled and chopped
1/3 cup olive oil	1 1/2 cups rice
2 medium cloves garlic	3–3 1/2 cups water
a large bunch of parsley, chopped very fine	pepper and salt to taste

Heat cleaned mussels and clams over a moderate fire; shake pan occasionally until they open. Remove shells, put shellfish aside, and strain the juice through a kitchen towel. Measure juice and put it aside. Put to boil in a separate pot enough water to make a total of 3¾ cups liquid.

Heat olive oil in a flat pan with the chopped garlic. When the garlic begins to take on color, put in the parsley, tomato, mussels, and clams. Let it all fry for 2 minutes. Add shellfish juice. As soon as the juice begins to boil, add the rice, seasoning, and boiling water. Cook over high flame until the rice begins to absorb the liquid. Reduce flame and cook 10–15 minutes longer or until rice is done. Let it rest 3–4 minutes before serving.

ARROZ ABANDA
(*A TWO-COURSE RICE*)

SERVINGS: 6

Abanda means "apart" in the Valencian dialect, and this rice, which is popular in Valencia and Alicante, is served alone as a first course, followed by the fish that gave the rice its flavor. The following recipe is from the Gayango restaurant in Madrid, which has internationalized the fish sauce in a delicious way. In Valencia, the fish is usually served with All-i-oli (pp. 188–191).

3 lbs. fish and shellfish (shrimp, clams, mussels, squid, lobster, sea bass)
5 cups water or fish stock
2/3 cup olive oil
1/2 head of garlic

2 cups rice
1/3 cup peeled, seeded, chopped tomatoes
a squirt of dry white wine
a pinch of paprika
a sprig of parsley, chopped

FISH SAUCE

1/2 cup olive oil
2 garlic cloves
2 egg yolks
3 small tomatoes
1 tsp sugar

a dash of tabasco sauce
a dash of Worcestershire sauce
a few drops of lemon juice

salt to taste

Cover the cleaned fish and shellfish with cold water (or fish stock if you have it). The amount of liquid should be no less than 5 cups. Bring it to a boil and simmer until the fish is cooked through and the mollusks have all opened. Strain fish and set aside, saving liquid.

Brown garlic over a low fire in 2/3 cup olive oil. Add parsley, paprika, and tomato in quick succession. Force the resulting mixture through a sieve onto 2 cups of raw rice and brown the rice in the olive oil for 3–5 minutes. Bring 5 cups of the liquid in which the fish cooked to a boil and pour it into the rice. Cook over a high fire for about 10 minutes. The rice will bubble at first; when it begins to make a popping noise, reduce flame and cook 10 minutes more on slow fire. Sprinkle white wine on top of rice and cook briefly on even hotter fire than at first. The rice should be so dry that you can tilt the pan on its side without having a grain fall out.

Serve the rice first, alone or decorated with a few mussels and clams. As a second course, serve the fish, cooled, with All-i-oli (pp. 188–191) or the following sauce:

Pound two garlic cloves in a mortar, pour in a little of the ½ cup of olive oil, add the two egg yolks, and mix until thick. Fry the tomatoes, whole, and peel them. Little by little, add the rest of the olive oil, the fried tomato, and the sugar. Season with salt, tabasco, Worcestershire, and a few drops of lemon juice. The finished sauce should have the consistency of a mayonnaise.

ARROZ CON COSTRADO DE HUEVOS ESTILO ALICANTE
(CRUSTED RICE ALICANTE STYLE)

SERVINGS: 6

1 small chicken	*2 TB olive oil*
½ lb. cured ham	*½ small onion, minced*
2 small chorizo (*or pepperoni*) *sausages*	*1 pork sausage*
1 cup dried chick-peas, soaked overnight in water	*1 blood sausage (optional)*
8 cups cold water	*2 cups rice*
	salt and pepper to taste
	3 eggs

Put chicken, cleaned and quartered, in a deep pot with the ham, *chorizos,* and chick-peas. Add 8 cups cold water and bring to a boil over a moderate flame. Reduce and simmer steadily, uncovered, until chick-peas are tender (1½–3 hours). Season to taste when cooked.

When chick-peas are tender, start preparing rice. Heat

2 TB olive oil in a flat pan or casserole with low sides. Fry the whole pork sausage with the minced onion. When the latter is browned, fry the whole blood sausage lightly. Remove sausages and slice them. Slice *chorizo,* ham, and chicken. Brown rice in pan for 2–3 minutes. Add sliced sausages, ham, chicken, and chick-peas. Measure out 5 cups of liquid from the pot in which the chick-peas cooked and add it, boiling hot, to the rice. Stir to mix and let it boil fast for a few minutes over a high flame. When you see that the rice is beginning to absorb the liquid, moderate the fire and continue cooking 10–15 minutes longer. When the rice has absorbed all the liquid, test it. If not yet done, add a small quantity of boiling liquid from the chick-pea stock and continue cooking. When rice is done, quickly beat three eggs until foamy and pour them over the rice. Put dish in hot oven for a few minutes until eggs puff and brown. Remove and let rest 3–4 minutes before serving.

ARROZ CON COSTA AL ESTILO DE ELCHE
(RICE WITH OVEN-BROWNED CRUST ELCHE STYLE)

SERVINGS: 6

1 cup dried chick-peas, soaked overnight in water	*¼ cup olive oil*
	1 small, tender chicken
3 pork sausages	*1 garlic clove, chopped*
1 small onion	*2 cups rice*
1 bay leaf	*3 eggs*
8 cups cold water	*salt and pepper*

Put chick-peas to cook in a large pot with one of the pork sausages, the onion, bay leaf, and 8 cups of cold water. Let it come to a boil slowly and then simmer steadily until the chick-peas are done (1½–3 hours).

When the chick-peas are half cooked, fry the remaining pork sausages in ¼ cup olive oil. Remove them and fry the chicken, cut in small pieces, dried, and seasoned with salt and pepper. When the chicken is well browned, fry the chopped garlic clove. Replace pork sausage and add enough liquid from the chick-peas to cover the sausage and chicken. Let the mixture cook slowly 35–45 minutes or until chicken is cooked through, but not soft.

Remove chicken to shallow pan or casserole. Add 5 cups of boiling liquid from the cooking of the chick-peas. Bring it to a rapid boil again before adding the rice. Add the cooked, drained chick-peas, season to taste, stir once to mix, and boil over a high flame for a few minutes until the rice begins to absorb the liquid. Cut the sausage into slices and distribute it on top of the rice while you continue cooking over a reduced flame for an additional 10–15 minutes, or until the rice is done. Beat three eggs with a little salt until fluffy, spread them over the surface of the rice, and immediately put it in a hot oven until it has formed a good crust. Remove rice and let it rest 3–4 minutes before serving.

ARROZ CON POLLITOS MERCEDES
(MOLDED RICE WITH CHICKEN)

SERVINGS: 4–6

20 *small pitted olives*	*salt and white pepper*
2 *young, very tender*	1 TB *tomato purée*
chickens	3¾ *cups canned*
4 TB *olive oil*	*chicken soup or stock*
4 TB *butter*	*made with chicken*
½ *cup dry white wine*	*bouillon cubes*

1 medium onion, chopped
¼ lb. cured ham, cut in strips
1½ cups rice
2 oz. grated Swiss or Dutch cheese

Simmer olives in water to cover for 5 minutes; drain and set aside. Cut each chicken in four pieces, dry them well, sprinkle them with salt, and fry them over a hot fire in 2 TB olive oil and 2 TB butter. When chicken is browned, add white wine and a pinch of pepper. When the wine has reduced to half, add the tomato purée (first mixing it with a little of the juice). Mix in the olives, add salt to taste, cover the casserole, and cook very slowly until the chicken is tender. Add a little water during cooking if necessary to thin sauce.

Preheat oven to 400° and bring the chicken stock to boil on the side. In a flat casserole, heat 2 TB olive oil with 2 TB butter. Fry the chopped onion with the ham cut in strips. When the onion turns golden, add the rice. Brown the rice. Pour boiling chicken stock over rice, quickly mix in cheese, check seasoning, and put dish in 400° oven for about 15 minutes or until the rice is done.

Take a crown mold, butter it, pack the mold with the rice, let it rest a few minutes, then unmold it in a large, round dish. Arrange the chicken in the center with the olives and ham on top. Pour chicken sauce over both rice and chicken and serve.

CHAPTER 8

EMPANADAS
(PASTRIES)
AND NOODLES

EMPANADAS and the smaller empanadillas—pastries with fillings of fish, meat, vegetables, or a combination of these—are popular all over Spain. From the Empanada Gallega, which is a full and hearty meal, to little empanadillas sold and eaten on the street, there are fillings and doughs to suit every taste. On the basis of the recipes given in this chapter, you can easily invent your own versions, adapting the size of the pastries to the occasion and the contents to what you have in the cupboard and the icebox. Bun-sized empanadillas served with soup make a good light supper or lunch; tiny ones make delicious cocktail

108

tidbits; loaf-size empanadas are a good picnic meal.

Noodles are not Spanish in origin, but they were introduced from Italy long enough ago to permit the development of a Spanish way of preparing them quite unlike anything to be found in Italy. Catalan Noodles make an excellent and economical buffet supper dish totally distinct from the usual noodle dishes.

EMPANADA GALLEGA
(GALICIAN STUFFED PASTRY)

The empanada is served hot or cold and is a favorite for meals eaten in the fields. It is made with a variety of fillings, and while sometimes served as a first course, is usually considered a meal. This version is definitely to be considered a meal.

SERVINGS: 10

5 cups flour
½ cup butter
2 eggs
1 tsp baking powder
1 tsp salt
1 cup cold water
⅔ cup lard
4 medium onions, chopped
salt and ground black pepper to taste

½ lb. chorizo (or pepperoni) sasuage
1 lb. pork
½ lb. cured ham
½ lb. veal
a pinch of saffron
1 hot chili pepper (or a pinch of cayenne pepper)
1 egg yolk, mixed with 1 TB water and 1 stigma saffron

Put flour on a table or marble slab. Make a hole in the center for the baking powder, butter, salt, water, and eggs.

109

Blend well with hands until it makes a cohesive mass which does not stick to the fingers. Let dough rest in a warm place in a bowl covered with a damp cloth while preparing the filling.

Heat lard. Fry onion very slowly in large, covered frying pan. Before onion takes on color, add *chorizo* (or pepperoni), skinned and cut in slices; pork, ham, and veal in small cubes; minced chili pepper, and a pinch of saffron previously ground in a mortar or bowl. Season mixture with salt and ground black pepper. Cover it and cook slowly about 45 minutes or until all meat is tender.

Preheat oven to 450°. Divide dough in two and roll each part out on lightly floured surface. Lift one piece of rolled dough carefully onto greased baking sheet. Put all the filling on it except for 2 TB of the liquid which should be reserved for later use. Leave a ½ inch margin around the edges of the dough. Lift the second piece over the filling, seal by pressing edges together, and brush top of pastry with an egg yolk beaten with 1 TB cold water and a stigma of crushed saffron. Make an air hole the thickness of a pencil in the middle of the dough. Bake pastry approximately 15 minutes in a 450° oven. When it is browned, remove it, and pour through the air hole the 2 TB of liquid reserved.

NOTE: In Galicia, it is customary to put aside a small ball of dough to decorate the top of the empanada with a design or initials before baking.

EMPANADILLAS VALENCIANAS
(*VALENCIAN TURNOVERS*)

These pastries can be stuffed with any of a variety of fillings. Recipes for ham and tuna fillings are given below.

PASTRY

SERVINGS: 10 turnovers

3 cups flour
½ cup olive oil
½ cup cold water
1 tsp salt

1 tsp anise liqueur (if not available, substitute a pinch of ground anise seed)

Put flour on a table or marble slab. Make a hole in the center for the remaining ingredients. Mix dough thoroughly with fingers, roll into a ball, and allow to rest while you prepare the filling.

HAM FILLING

3 small onions, chopped
2 small tomatoes, peeled and chopped
1 clove garlic, minced

2 thick slices cured ham, diced
2 hard-boiled eggs
3 TB olive oil
salt and pepper to taste

Heat olive oil in a skillet and slowly fry the onions. When they are soft and golden, add tomatoes and garlic. When the liquid has evaporated, add diced ham, stir and fry 2–3 minutes more. Remove from fire, add mashed hard-boiled eggs, and season with salt and pepper.

TUNA FILLING

2 medium onions, chopped
2 medium tomatoes, peeled and chopped

2 hard-boiled eggs
⅓ cup olive oil
1 7-oz. can of tuna
salt to taste

Heat olive oil to the verge of smoking. Fry chopped onions slowly. When they are golden, add tomatoes. Let

111

liquid from tomatoes evaporate before adding mashed hard-boiled eggs and tuna broken into bits. Mix well, fry briefly; add salt if necessary.

BAKING

1 beaten egg

Preheat oven to 425°. Roll out dough fairly thin (¼ inch or less) and cut out ten circles about 6 inches in diameter. Fill half of each circle. Leave a small margin along the circumference. Fold the other half over the filling, pinch edges to close in a fluted pattern, brush with beaten egg, prick top with fork, and bake on greased sheet for 25 minutes or until browned and crisp.

NOTE: If you have dough left, store in the refrigerator for use in Cocktail Empanadillas (pp. 48–49) or Fried Banana Pastries (p. 212).

EMPAREDADOS CALIENTES
(HOT SANDWICHES)

SERVINGS: 4

8 *slices slightly stale*	8 *slices lean ham*
bread (3–4 days old)	¼ *cup olive oil*
1 *cup milk*	*salt and pepper*
2 *beaten eggs*	

Put milk in a shallow dish and with the aid of a fork, dip bread in it until the bread is dampened but not soaked. Fold each piece of bread over a slice of ham and put all the sandwiches between two cutting boards under a heavy weight for half an hour. (If you have a stone mortar, that is a very effective weight.) Dip the sandwiches in eggs beaten with salt and pepper and fry in hot olive oil until well browned. Serve hot.

112

TALLARINES A LA CATALANA
(*CATALAN NOODLES IN SAUCE*)

SERVINGS: 6

1 *lb. egg noodles*
1 *lb. pork spare ribs cut in pieces 2" long*
18 *slices cooked pork sausage*
½ *lb. lean salt pork, cubed*
1 *large onion, chopped fine*
3 *medium tomatoes, peeled and chopped*
2 *medium cloves garlic, minced*

15 *peeled toasted almonds*
3 TB *pine nuts (add almonds if pine nuts are unavailable)*
several sprigs parsley
11 *cups boiling meat stock or beef bouillon*
3 TB *olive oil*
ground black pepper
salt to taste

Brown spare ribs in 3 TB olive oil in a large casserole with cubed salt pork. Add minced garlic and chopped onion. When onion is golden and soft, add peeled, chopped tomatoes. Fry until sauce thickens. Add boiling meat stock or beef bouillon and slices of cooked sausage; let it boil 5 minutes. In a mortar, pound the almonds, pine nuts, and parsley. Add a little liquid from the casserole to dissolve the paste, then pour the paste into the casserole. Mix well, add uncooked noodles, season with black pepper, stir, and boil slowly for 20 minutes or until noodles are done and sauce has thickened. Stir to prevent sticking, particularly toward end of cooking time. If meat stock or bouillon is salty, no more salt may be needed; check seasoning when cooking is almost completed. Serve in the casserole.

CHAPTER 9

FISH AND SHELLFISH

THE outstanding quality of the fish sold in Spain is its impeccable freshness. Unfortunately modern ways are being introduced rapidly, refrigeration now makes it possible to keep fish for sale days after it is caught, and frozen fish is beginning to appear in the Spanish markets. One cannot help thinking with nostalgia of Roman times when the law prevented fishmongers from sitting down until they had sold all their fish.*

Spain enjoys a variety of fish and shellfish, including some little known in other areas. Galicia and the southern coast near Cádiz are outstanding for fish and shellfish specialties. Some of Spain's seafood originated elsewhere:

* Marquesa de Parabere, *Historia de la Gastronomía,* Madrid: Espasa-Calpe, S.A., 1943.

114

the crayfish of Spain's southeastern Mediterranean coast, for example, are descendants of those Hannibal's brother, Hasdrubal, brought from Carthage over two thousand years ago.

Fresh fish has only the faintest, most delicate odor, which you can barely detect without sniffing. The gills are red; the eyes clear and not glassy; the flesh firm. Fish should always be cleaned as soon after being caught as possible and should then be washed. If fish is not recently caught, add lemon juice to the washing water. If fish is not to be used for several hours, store it, cleaned, washed, and lightly salted, in a cool place.

As in Portugal, salted cod is used in innumerable dishes. The Spanish have been fond of it since they began cod fishing in the ninth century, and cod was a staple fish in the interior before the invention of the railroad made fresh fish available everywhere. Before use, salted cod is soaked in water for about twelve hours, during which the water is changed several times. Properly desalted, it is a very fine white fish and a suitable base for sauces and seasonings of great variety. The French chef Escoffier found cod of sufficient interest to write a book giving eighty-two ways of preparing it. A number of cod recipes are included here, all of which can be made with another firm white fish (such as halibut) if you prefer.

CLEANING MUSSELS

Mussels should be alive when cooked. This means that their shells must either be closed or, if open, must close when touched. Avoid dead or cracked mussels when buying and discard any you find while cleaning.

As soon as you bring the mussels home, put them in a bowl or pail of cool water in a cool place and do not clean until you are about to cook them. If you must keep them overnight, cook them and store them in the refrigerator.

To clean, scrub mussels one by one to remove all dirt and seaweed. Scrape off any hard shell matter with an old knife and pull off the beard or tough hairs emerging from between the shells. The water should be changed during the cleaning frequently and until it remains clear. Careful cleaning will almost eliminate the possibility of gritty mussels or a sandy sauce.

COLD MUSSELS

Mussels to be served cold or stored overnight should be cooked in a saucepan over a moderate flame until all the mussels open. A wide-bottomed pan is preferable because it distributes the heat more evenly. Shake pan continuously until mussels have released enough juice to prevent burning the pan. As soon as all of them have opened, remove them; longer cooking will toughen them. A few minutes should suffice. If one or two stubbornly refuse to open, discard them as suspect.

COLD MUSSELS WITH ALMOND SAUCE
SERVINGS: 4–6

3–4 doz. cleaned mussels
8 peeled, toasted almonds
½ the center of a slice of white bread

½ cup olive oil
1 TB wine vinegar
salt and white pepper to taste

Cook mussels according to instructions for cold mussels (p. 116). Remove one shell from each and allow mussels to cool while you prepare the sauce.

Crush almonds in a mortar, add bread and pound it, then add vinegar, and, gradually, while stirring, the ½ cup olive oil. When it is mixed, season with salt and pepper to taste (some like this sauce very peppery). Pour sauce over mussels and allow dish to sit for about an hour before putting it in refrigerator to chill.

If you have an electric blender, put all ingredients of the sauce in it at once and mix until blended.

COLD MUSSELS WITH LEMON DRESSING
SERVINGS: 4–6

3–4 doz. cleaned mus-   9 TB olive oil
sels   black pepper to taste
3 TB lemon juice (or
vinegar)

Cook mussels according to instructions for cold mussels (p. 116). Remove one shell from each. Mix olive oil with lemon juice and pour it over mussels. Grind black pepper liberally over them. Wait 1 hour before putting mussels in refrigerator to chill.

MUSSELS IN TOMATO SAUCE
SERVINGS: 4–6

3–4 doz. cleaned mus-   1 recipe Tomato-
sels   Garlic Sauce (p. 194)

Prepare tomato sauce. While it thickens, cook mussels according to instructions for cold mussels (p. 116).

117

Remove one shell from each bivalve and pour thickened sauce over them. Serve hot or chill an hour or more in the refrigerator.

ALMEJAS A LA MARINERA
(*CLAMS IN WHITE WINE*)

SERVINGS: 4

6 *doz. small clams, cleaned*

2 *medium tomatoes, peeled and chopped*

1 *medium onion, minced*

½ *cup dry white wine*

1 *large bunch parsley, chopped*

5 TB *olive oil*

salt and white pepper to taste

Presoak clams for at least an hour in two changes of water in order to rid them of sand. Fry chopped onion slowly in hot olive oil until it begins to take on color; add tomatoes, and when sauce has thickened, season it with pepper and add clams with white wine. When clams have all opened, stir in chopped parsley, salt to taste, and serve.

TALLINAS A LA CATALANA
(*SMALL CLAMS IN SAUCE*)

SERVINGS: 6

4½ *lbs. small clams, cleaned*

4 *cloves garlic, peeled*

2 *medium tomatoes, peeled and chopped*

2 *sprigs of parsley, chopped*

juice of ¼ lemon

3 TB *olive oil*

1 *heaping* TB *butter*

salt and pepper to taste

118

Heat olive oil until barely simmering; fry minced garlic over low fire. When garlic begins to take on color, add tomato. After tomato liquid has reduced, put in chopped parsley and clams, carefully cleaned and previously soaked at least 1 hour in cold water. Cover dish and cook over low fire until all clams are open, giving dish an occasional shake to stir it. Squeeze lemon over clams, stir in butter, season with pepper and salt to taste, and serve.

MARISCADA A LA MARINERA
(ASSORTED BAKED SHELLFISH)

SERVINGS: 6

3 doz. small clams, cleaned

3 doz. mussels, cleaned

1 medium-large onion, minced

1 small tomato, peeled, seeded, and chopped

1 small clove garlic, minced

3 TB olive oil

1 rounded tsp flour

1 heaping TB chopped parsley

a pinch of ground pepper

Preheat oven to 400°. Put cleaned shellfish in a saucepan and shake gently over moderate heat for 3–4 minutes until they open. Remove shellfish to ovenproof pan. Strain juice through kitchen towel and reserve for later use.

Slowly fry minced onion in 3 TB hot olive oil. Add tomato when onion begins to take on color. After liquid from tomato has evaporated, add minced garlic clove, chopped parsley, and flour. Stir to prevent burning while flour cooks for 1 minute. Pour in liquid reserved from cooking of shellfish. Add pepper. Boil sauce for 1–2 minutes while stirring. Pour sauce over shellfish and bake in 400° oven 6–7 minutes.

NOTE: Mariscada a la Marinera can be made with any assortment of shellfish locally available. If you use large-shelled seafood, you may wish to remove one shell from each mollusk before covering with sauce. The recipe is Galician, and the version given above is from the Hogar Gallego in Madrid.

GAMBAS AL AJILLO
(*GARLIC SHRIMP*)

At the Gayango restaurant in Madrid, which provided the following recipe, each portion is served in a small earthenware casserole about 4 inches in diameter. The following amounts are for each such casserole. The number of shrimp depends on the size of the shrimp. The dish can also be made in one large, flat casserole; simply multiply the recipe by the number of people to be served.

SERVINGS: 1

*12 small shrimp,
   cleaned and deveined*
2 TB olive oil
3 cloves garlic
*a small piece of hot
   chili pepper (or a
   pinch of cayenne)*

½ bay leaf
a squirt of lemon
*a spoonful of All-i-oli
   (pp. 188–190)*
*a sprinkling of celery
   salt*

Brown three cloves garlic in 2 TB olive oil. Add chili pepper (or cayenne) and bay leaf. Put in the shrimp, turn once to brown both sides, add a spoonful of all-i-oli, squirt lightly with lemon juice, sprinkle with celery salt, and serve sizzling hot. The all-i-oli should remain intact or almost intact, the shrimp should be brown and slightly crusty, and the garlic cloves should remain whole. Small shrimp cook in very few minutes; take care not to overcook.

NOTE: Those who find chili pepper or cayenne too potent can omit it and grind black pepper over shrimp just before serving.

TOMATES RELLENOS RIA DE AROSA
(GALICIAN TOMATOES STUFFED WITH SHELLFISH)

SERVINGS: 6

12 medium tomatoes, ripe, firm, and as equal in size as possible	a scant ½ cup olive oil
	1 bay leaf
	⅛ tsp oregano
	⅛ tsp thyme
18 prawns or large shrimp, cleaned and deveined	¼ cup cognac
	1 egg
3 doz. small clams, cleaned	1 TB dry bread crumbs
	1 TB grated cheese
2 medium-large onions, chopped	1 sprig of parsley, chopped fine
¼ cup dry white wine	salt and pepper to taste

Wash and dry tomatoes. Cut a small lid from the top of each; scoop out tomato pulp and save it for later use. Remove heads and peel from raw shrimp. Crush heads

121

and peel in mortar. Cut shrimp into small pieces and sprinkle lightly with salt. Put cleaned clams in saucepan with ¼ cup white wine and let them steam open over moderate heat. When opened, remove them from fire, discard shells, and put clams aside, saving the liquid in which they cooked.

Heat 3 TB olive oil in a frying pan or earthenware casserole and slowly brown chopped onion with bay leaf, oregano, and thyme. When onion begins to turn golden, add tomato pulp and crushed heads and peel of shrimp. Let sauce reduce on very hot fire until tomato juice has evaporated, leaving a thick sauce. Pass sauce through sieve and set aside.

Heat 2 TB olive oil in a frying pan. Fry chopped shrimp briefly over hot fire. Almost at once, add the shelled clams and ¼ cup cognac, warmed in advance. Light cognac and let it burn. As soon as the alcohol has evaporated, mix in tomato sauce and a little of the liquid in which the clams cooked. (Pour with care to avoid getting sand into dish.) Let the sauce reduce on a hot fire until there is very little liquid. Remove from fire, season with salt and pepper, let it cool a moment, then rapidly blend in a beaten egg. (All of the foregoing can be prepared hours in advance.)

Twenty minutes before serving, preheat oven to 400°, place tomatoes on an ovenproof serving dish with sides, put a little salt inside each tomato, and fill it with shellfish mixture. Blend dry bread crumbs, cheese, and chopped parsley. Sprinkle over tops of tomatoes. Pour remaining olive oil over tomatoes and place them in upper part of 400° oven. Bake until warmed through and browned on top. Just before serving, baste with sauce formed during baking.

SHANGURRO (I)
(BASQUE STUFFED CRAB)

The giant crab of the Basques weighs 5 pounds or more. The following recipe, which is from Casa Nicolasa of San Sebastián requires live crab. It is served with plain boiled rice (p. 184).

SERVINGS: 4

4 *giant crabs*

2 *medium onions, minced*

2 *garlic cloves, minced*

5 TB *olive oil*

2 *ripe tomatoes, peeled and chopped*

¼ *cup butter*

2 TB *chopped parsley*

1 *cup dry white wine*

2 *tsp salt*

2 *tsp sugar*

a *pinch of cayenne pepper*

½ *cup dry bread crumbs*

Cook crabs by plunging them alive into boiling salt water (sea water if possible) and boiling them for half an hour. Let them cool. Remove all the meat, taking care not to mix in any small particles of shell. Save the body shells.

Fry minced onion and garlic very slowly in olive oil. When they begin to take on color, increase heat. Add tomato. Let liquid evaporate. Add parsley and wine. Cook over a hot fire for 2–3 minutes until alcohol has evaporated. Force all the juices and internal parts of the crabs through a colander. Blend the strained mixture into the sauce with salt, sugar, and cayenne. This much can be prepared in advance.

Before serving, heat crabmeat in sauce, fill cleaned

123

body shells of crab, sprinkle tops with bread crumbs, dot with butter, and brown in 400° oven.

SHANGURRO (II)
(*BASQUE STUFFED CRAB*)

Unlike the preceding recipe, this one can be made with canned crab.

SERVINGS: 1

1 *live hard-shelled crab (or ¼ lb. canned crab)*	¼ *tsp paprika*
	2 TB *olive oil*
	¼ *cup cognac*
½ *medium onion, chopped*	1 TB *butter*
½ *garlic clove, chopped*	1–2 TB *dry bread crumbs*
1 *very small tomato, peeled and chopped*	

Hard-shelled crab is cooked like lobster: plunged live into boiling salted water to cover. Use sea water if available; if not, add a little green vegetable to the cooking water. Boil crab 15 minutes. Remove and allow to cool.

To clean, break off claws, remove back, and scrape out all spongy parts underneath. Cut out small apron-shaped section on underside of crab. Crack legs and scrape out meat. Remove meat from shell; drain out and save any juice. The foregoing can be done in advance of cooking if more convenient.

Heat olive oil, fry chopped onion; when onion turns golden, brown garlic clove. Add tomato. Off the fire, stir in paprika. Return to fire. Pour in cognac and let alcohol evaporate. Add juice from crab shell (or can) and crabmeat. Fill crab shell with mixture, dot with butter, sprinkle with bread crumbs, and put in top part of hot oven for about 10 minutes or until browned. If you have not used live crab, substitute individual ramekins or scallop shells for crab shell.

CALAMARES A LA ROMANA
(BATTER FRIED SQUID)
SERVINGS: 6

6 small to medium squid	½ cup flour
	¾ cup olive oil
2 beaten eggs	a pinch of salt

Wash cleaned squid; remove tentacles; dry fish thoroughly. Cut body of squid into rings, dip them in flour, then in egg beaten with a pinch of salt. Fry rings in very hot oil. The fish is done as soon as it is browned on all sides. Frying time should in no case exceed 5 minutes because squid toughens when overcooked.

NOTE: The tentacles can be used as well as the body of the squid if you like. Slices of hake or any other white fish can be fried in the same way.

ATUN A LO VASCO
(TUNA STEAKS BAKED WITH TOMATO)
SERVINGS: 6

6 large fresh tuna steaks (¾" thick)	1 cup dry white wine
1 large onion, chopped	a branch of thyme (or ½ tsp dried thyme)
4 medium tomatoes, peeled and seeded	1 TB sugar
2 cloves garlic, minced	⅓ cup olive oil
	salt and pepper to taste

125

Preheat oven to 400°. Fry *unwashed* tuna steaks in ⅓ cup very hot olive oil. Salt and pepper steaks liberally while frying. When browned on both sides, put in a baking dish. Pour in white wine until it reaches the middle of the steaks (about 1 cup).

Reheat the oil in which you browned the tuna. Slowly fry the chopped onion until golden with thyme branch. Add minced garlic cloves. When garlic is beginning to take on color, put in tomatoes, peeled, seeded, and cut in quarters. Salt to taste. Mix in sugar. When tomatoes are barely cooked, pour sauce over tuna. Bake in 400° oven for 1 hour, basting with sauce during baking.

BACALAO PIL-PIL
(*COD SIMMERED WITH GARLIC AND PARSLEY*)
SERVINGS: 6

12 pieces desalted cod about 2" x 3"	*4 cloves garlic, peeled*
	2 TB chopped parsley
⅓ cup olive oil	

Put cod in hot water on very slow fire for 2½ hours. When cod has softened, remove bones and return it to hot water. Crush four garlic cloves and chop very fine. Put them to fry very slowly in ⅓ cup olive oil in a flat earthenware casserole. When the garlic takes on color, add parsley. Remove casserole from fire until the oil is just barely sizzling. Return to fire to add drained pieces of cod. Increase heat. Shake the casserole and give it a twist from time to time. Five minutes after putting in cod, turn fish over. When it has been cooking in the oil 10 minutes, add 2 TB of the water in which the cod cooked previously. Continue cooking for another 5 minutes; shake casserole from time to time to blend. By then, the gelatinous juices of the cod will have combined with the olive oil to make a sauce the consistency of a thin cream sauce. Serve immediately.

BACALAO A LA VIZCAINA
(BISCAYAN COD)

SERVINGS: 6

2 lbs. desalted cod
1 large onion, minced
4 medium cloves garlic, minced
3 TB olive oil
1 medium potato, minced

5 dried red peppers, soaked in water overnight
1 large ripe tomato, peeled and seeded
1 bay leaf

Put desalted cod on fire with water to cover. Remove as soon as it boils; strain, reserving water. Let fish cool. Debone and cut in serving pieces. Slowly fry minced onion and garlic in olive oil until brown. Open soaked peppers, discard seeds, and scrape off pulp from inside. Add pulp to fried onions and garlic. Spread minced potato over bottom of casserole containing onion and garlic. Pour over it the tomato passed through a sieve. Place the boned cod in the casserole, skin side up, and barely cover with some of the water in which the cod cooked. Add bay leaf. Simmer approximately 45 minutes or until sauce has reduced and thickened slightly. From time to time, move the casserole to mix the sauce and add more of the water in which the cod cooked if necessary.

NOTE: This dish is even better if made the day before and reheated.

COD IN TOMATO SAUCE

SERVINGS: 4–6

2 lbs. desalted cod cut in serving pieces

½ cup olive oil

1 large onion, chopped fine

3 ripe tomatoes or 1½ cups canned tomato

2 cloves garlic

flour

Heat olive oil to the verge of smoking in a skillet. Dip pieces of cod in flour and fry lightly on both sides. Remove to a plate.

In the same oil, fry the onion slowly until it is yellow and soft. Fry tomatoes, peeled and chopped, over a moderate flame until the sauce has thickened. Add two cloves of pressed or crushed garlic, cook 2 minutes longer, reheat cod in sauce, and serve.

COD CROQUETTES

SERVINGS: 12 medium croquettes

¾ cup boned, skinned, desalted cod

2 TB olive oil

4 slightly rounded TB flour

¼ cup minced onion

2 TB chopped parsley

1½ cups milk

1 egg

a mixture of 5 TB dry bread crumbs and 2 TB flour for rolling croquettes

½–¾ cup olive oil for frying

Cook minced onion slowly in 2 TB olive oil in a saucepan. When onion is golden, add cod squeezed of

128

liquid and cut into small pieces. After all remaining liquid has cooked out, stir in chopped parsley and 4 rounded TB flour. When mixture is entirely dry, remove from stove and stir with a wooden spoon while gradually adding 1½ cups cold milk. Return pan to fire and cook over moderate heat 20–30 minutes until there is no taste of raw flour and mixture is a thick paste. You will have to stir more and more frequently to prevent sticking as the paste thickens. Remove from fire, blend in an egg yolk (reserving the white for later use), and allow to cool thoroughly. This much can be prepared in advance, even the previous day.

Stir egg white just enough to blend. Spread mixture of bread crumbs and flour on plate, board, or table. With wet hands, make evenly shaped small croquettes out of the dough, dipping each in the egg white, then rolling it in the mixture of bread crumbs and flour.

In a large skillet, heat enough olive oil to cover the pan to a depth of ¼ inch (½–¾ cup). Fry croquettes gently, taking care to brown them evenly. Remove, drain on paper, and serve.

NOTE: Unlike most foods, these are best served warm, not hot. Bite-size croquettes served on toothpicks are excellent with cocktails.

LANGOSTA DEL POBRE (I)
(POOR MAN'S LOBSTER)
SERVINGS: 4

This dish can be made with the tail part of any firm white fish. Ask to have the piece skinned, boned, and tied with a string like a small roast. Save the spiny piece to enrich the sauce. Although the recipe calls for a fairly large amount of garlic, the garlic flavor is not pronounced.

tail part of any white   *1 bay leaf*
  fish (about 2 lbs.)   *2–3 medium carrots*
4–5 cloves of garlic   *2* TB *paprika*
         2 TB *olive oil*

Wash and dry fish. Mash garlic cloves and anoint fish with the mashed garlic and olive oil. Roll it in paprika. Put it in an earthenware casserole with bay leaf and sliced carrots. Let it cook slowly, covered, approximately 30 minutes or until cooked through. Remove fish to warmed serving dish and untie string. Force sauce through a sieve and pour over fish.

The string will leave white marks on the pink-surfaced fish and will contribute to its resemblance to lobster.

LANGOSTA DEL POBRE (II)
(POOR MAN'S LOBSTER)
SERVINGS: 4

tail part of any white fish prepared as for the preceding recipe (total weight approximately 2 lbs.)
milk to cover
2 TB *paprika*

Wash and dry fish. Roll in paprika. Place in saucepan, cover with cold milk, and simmer on slow fire until fish is cooked through (15 minutes or less). Serve hot or cold. If cold, serve with Mayonnaise (p. 191), All-i-oli (pp. 189–191), or Romesco Sauce (p. 193).

130

LENGUADO CON SALSA DE NUECES
(SOLE IN NUT SAUCE)

SERVINGS: 4

4 center slices or 4 fillets of sole or any delicately flavored white fish

10 blanched almonds

15 hazelnuts

2 TB pine nuts

1 TB chopped parsley

a small pinch of saffron

1 small clove garlic

½ slice melba toast or a small piece of dry, toasted bread

salt to taste

Grind in a mortar or electric blender the almonds, hazelnuts, pine nuts, toast, parsley, saffron, and garlic. Put fish in saucepan with enough cold water to cover. Simmer for a few minutes until fish is just cooked through; watch closely. Drain fish and put in flat pan or casserole. Gradually add to the nut mixture enough of the water in which the fish cooked to make a sauce of the consistency of a light cream sauce. Mix well. Salt to taste. Pour sauce over fish, let it bubble once or twice over a medium flame, and serve at once.

NOTE: Nut sauce is very delicate and best suited to fine white fish.

MERLUZA A LA GALLEGA
(HAKE WITH POTATOES AND ONION)

This has a subtle flavor; for those fond of garlic, the maximum amount will not be too much. The following recipe was provided by the Hogar Gallego in Madrid.

131

SERVINGS: 4

4 *large center slices of hake or other white fish*	3–5 *cloves of garlic, minced*
3 *medium potatoes, sliced thin*	2 *cups water*
1 *small onion, sliced thin*	¼ *cup olive oil*
	½ *tsp paprika*
	a small pinch of salt

Put 2 cups of water to boil with a small pinch of salt in a flat, fairly wide dish. Boil sliced onion and potatoes covered for 20 minutes or until almost tender. Add fish slices and reduce flame. The fish and vegetables should be covered with water: add a little boiling water if necessary. Replace lid and simmer on very low fire until fish is done (about 8 minutes for hake).

When the fish is cooked, pour off all liquid and reserve for use in a recipe calling for fish stock. In a skillet, heat ¼ cup olive oil. Fry minced garlic until brown. Remove skillet from fire to stir in paprika. The oil should be hot when it is added, but if too hot, the paprika will burn and give the dish a bitter taste. Pour oil over casserole containing fish and vegetables. Reheat for 2–3 minutes before serving.

MERLUZA A LO JAIZKIBEL
(*HAKE IN RICH SAUCE*)

This recipe is the creation of Señor Candido Tojal Varela, chef of the newly opened restaurant of the Hotel San Sebastián in the town of the same name. Because it is both simple and rich, the dish, which won the chef a prize in the First Gastronomic Competition of the Province of Guipuzcoa, should become one of the classics of the

Basque cuisine. The proportions in the following recipe are for two people; a double recipe for four would be best made simultaneously in two casseroles of equal size.

SERVINGS: 2

4 *serving pieces of fillet of hake or other white fish*	¼ *cup dry white wine*
8 *clams, cleaned*	2 *heaping* TB *green peas, canned or pre-cooked*
2 TB *olive oil*	4 *canned white asparagus tips*
2 *medium garlic cloves, peeled*	1 TB *juice from canned asparagus*
1 *heaping* TB *flour*	*yolk of 1 egg*
1 *rounded* TB *chopped parsley*	*salt to taste*

½ *cup water*

Heat olive oil in a flat earthenware casserole. Crush and mince garlic cloves. Fry slowly in the barely heated oil. When they take on color, add the flour, parsley, and hake, in that order. Jiggle the casserole to mix. In another receptacle, open six clams in ½ cup water over a hot fire. As soon as the clams have opened, turn the hake over, sprinkle it with white wine, remove a shell from each clam, and add the clams to the casserole with about a tablespoon of the water in which the clams cooked. Jiggle and shake the casserole to blend. Add the peas and asparagus tips. Season with salt and shake casserole to blend.

When the sauce has taken on the consistency of a cream sauce, put the yolk of an egg in a cup, add to it 1 TB of the juice from the can of asparagus, and mix it with a fork. Remove casserole from fire. Empty contents of cup over casserole and immediately lift casserole and swirl and shake it from side to side to blend the egg yolk with the sauce quickly. The dish is now ready to serve.

MERLUZA KOSKERA
(HAKE IN PEPPERY WINE SAUCE)

SERVINGS: 4

4 thick center slices of hake (or other white fish)
16 clams, cleaned
3 TB *olive oil*
4 medium garlic cloves, peeled
4 small pieces of dried chili pepper or a pinch of powdered cayenne
3 TB *flour*

a large handful of chopped parsley
½ cup dry white wine
2 tsp sherry
½ cup cooked or canned peas
8 asparagus stalks
2 hard-boiled eggs cut in half lengthwise
¼ cup meat stock or beef bouillon

salt to taste

Heat olive oil in a flat earthenware casserole while you crush and mince the garlic cloves. Fry them until golden brown. Regulate heat so that oil is just barely sizzling. Add chili pepper or cayenne, flour, parsley, fish, and clams in rapid succession. Jiggle casserole once to mix and cover it. One minute later, shake casserole again and turn fish over. One minute later, add white wine, sherry, and bouillon. Shake casserole to blend. Pour in peas, arrange asparagus in pairs, and place halves of hard-boiled eggs decoratively in casserole. Salt to taste. Shake and swirl to mix. Cook until the bone in the middle of the fish steaks is loose (a very few minutes).

134

MERLUZA A LA MARINERA
(HAKE IN ALMOND SAUCE)

The recipe for this classic Catalan dish and for the following Merluza Romesco come from the Restaurante Pi in Vendrell (Tarragona).

SERVINGS: 6

6 *center slices of hake, haddock, or other white fish*
1 *small onion, minced*
1 *medium tomato, peeled and chopped*
4 TB *olive oil*
16 *peeled, toasted almonds*

a piece approximately 3" x 3" of the center of a slice of white bread
4 *garlic cloves, peeled*
several sprigs of fresh parsley
salt to taste

Heat olive oil in a large frying pan or flat casserole. Fry minced onion until golden. Brown bread and remove it. Add peeled and chopped tomato. While the tomato fries gently with the onion until the liquid evaporates, bring the fish slices to a boil in a separate pan with enough water to cover. As soon as the water begins to boil, lower heat and simmer slowly until fish is cooked through. (Hake will take 5 minutes or less to cook.) Remove fish to a plate and reserve the liquid.

In a mortar or an electric blender, crush and mix the almonds, fried bread, garlic cloves, and parsley. (If you use a blender, add a few tablespoons of water.) When the paste is well blended, stir it into the tomato and onion mixture. Pour in enough water from the cooking of the

135

fish to thin the sauce and increase the quantity. Stir sauce, salt to taste, put fish in casserole, and boil sauce gently for 2 minutes while spooning the liquid over the fish. Serve immediately.

MERLUZA ROMESCO
(*HAKE IN PEPPERY SAUCE*)
SERVINGS: 6

1 recipe Merluza a la Marinera (p. 135)
1 rounded TB *flour*
several sprigs of parsley

½ hot chili pepper (substitute powdered cayenne if chile pepper is not available)
3 TB *olive oil*

Prepare Merluza a la Marinera. A few minutes before serving, crush chili pepper and parsley in mortar with flour. Blend in olive oil and pour into fish casserole. Stir sauce over low fire for 2–3 minutes and serve.

MERLUZA EN SALSA VERDE
(*HAKE WITH PARSLEY AND PEAS*)
SERVINGS: 2

2 TB *olive oil*
2 medium garlic cloves, minced
2 thick (¾") slices of hake or other white fish
14 cleaned small clams
1 TB *flour*
a pinch of salt

3 heaping TB *green peas, canned or precooked*
6 white asparagus tips canned or precooked
1 hard-boiled egg cut in half lengthwise
2 TB *water*
1 heaping TB *chopped parsley*

136

Heat oil in a flat earthenware casserole. Fry minced garlic cloves slowly. Flatten fish slices to ½-inch thickness. Add them when garlic has browned slightly; be certain oil is barely sizzling when fish is added. Sprinkle salt and flour over casserole and jiggle casserole to blend. Turn fish over. Add raw clams, sprinkle with peas, place asparagus stalks in threes on opposite sides of dish. Put halves of hard-boiled egg opposite each other. Pour in 2 TB water. Shake casserole gently to blend sauce. Cover dish and cook 15–20 minutes or until fish is just tender on a low fire, shaking casserole from time to time. Just before serving, sprinkle with chopped parsley.

MERLUZA A LO VASCO
(HAKE WITH SHRIMP)

SERVINGS: 4

4 *thick center slices of hake*

2 *doz. very small shrimp, cleaned and peeled*

4 *small potatoes, peeled*

4 *medium cloves garlic, peeled*

4 *small pieces of dried chili pepper or a dash of powdered cayenne* (*optional*)

a handful of chopped parsley

3 TB *olive oil*

½ *cup dry white wine*

4 *tsp sherry*

¼ *cup meat stock or beef bouillon*

8 *white asparagus tips, cooked or canned*

salt to taste

Heat olive oil in a flat earthenware casserole. Crush and mince garlic cloves. Fry over moderate heat until golden brown. Regulate heat so that oil is barely simmering before adding the potatoes. These are cut in small, thin slices (rather shavings than slices) and spread over the bottom of the casserole. Immediately put in the chili pepper or cayenne, the parsley, fish slices, and shrimp. Jiggle the casserole to mix. Cook for 1 minute. Add wine, sherry, bouillon or stock, asparagus stalks, and salt to taste. Jiggle and swirl the casserole to mix. Within a few minutes, the bone in the middle of the fish steak will be loose, indicating that the fish is done and the dish ready to serve.

MERO A LA BILBAINA
(HALIBUT WITH PEPPERS)

SERVINGS: 6

6 thick (½-lb.) slices hake or other white fish

1 medium-large onion, chopped

3 large garlic cloves, minced

3 large red peppers, seeded and minced

juice of ½ large lemon

1 bay leaf

5 TB olive oil

salt and pepper to taste

Heat olive oil in frying pan. Brown onion and garlic. Fry peppers until mixture reduces to a pulp. Sprinkle fish slices with salt, put in baking dish greased with olive oil. Pour lemon juice and a thin stream of olive oil over fish and bake in preheated 325° oven, basting occasionally.

When pepper-onion-garlic mixture has reduced to a pulp, add a little of the juice from the baking fish, season with salt and pepper, add bay leaf, and continue cooking the purée another 5 minutes. Pass it through a sieve, cover the fish with the purée, and continue baking until fish is done (a total of 20–30 minutes).

NOTE: You can increase the quantity of purée by the addition of fish stock if you choose.

RAPE AL JEREZ
(*WHITE FISH IN SHERRY SAUCE*)

Rape is not to be found in North America, but any firm white fish can be substituted.

SERVINGS: 4

4 *large center slices of*	¼ *cup sherry*
white fish, washed	1 *tsp lemon juice*
and dried	*a pinch of salt*
2 *egg yolks*	*a pinch of cinnamon*
5 TB *butter*	*pepper to taste*

Preheat oven to 350°. Flatten fish slices to an even thickness of a little more than ¼ inch. Salt them very lightly and place in a buttered, shallow ovenproof dish or casserole. Dot each slice with butter; reserve 2 TB for later use. Pour sherry over fish and bake in oven until cooked through (6–7 minutes).

While fish is baking, beat egg yolks in a saucepan with cinnamon, pepper, and 2 TB melted butter. Remove baked fish from oven, drain sauce from casserole into a bowl, and set fish in a warm place. Gradually add fish sauce to egg yolks while stirring constantly over a very low flame. Continue stirring until sauce thickens. Do not allow it to come to a boil. When it is the thickness of a good hollandaise, add lemon juice, stir, and pour sauce over fish. Reheat fish for 2–3 minutes in oven and serve in the same dish.

NOTE: To be successful, this recipe requires a certain speed and facility in the few minutes before serving. If you are not accustomed to using egg yolks to thicken a sauce, do not undertake it for large numbers before a preliminary trial. The dish can be made in small individual casseroles if you prefer.

An excellent addition is four or five clams per person, opened apart in a pan shaken over a moderate fire. Strain the juice from the clams and add it to the sauce. Remove clams from their shells. Put them in the dish just before it is reheated in the oven.

TRUCHA A LA NAVARRA
(*TROUT STUFFED WITH HAM*)

SERVINGS: 6

6 *trout of approximately* *flour for dusting*
½ lb. each, cleaned *3 whole garlic cloves*
with the smallest pos- *approximately ¾ cup*
sible opening *olive oil for frying*
6 *slices cured ham, cut* *salt*
thin

Heat olive oil in a large skillet with three whole garlic cloves until the garlic is browned. Discard garlic and save oil for frying trout.

Through the opening at the gills of the fish, stuff a thin, rolled piece of cured ham. Sprinkle fish with salt, dust lightly in flour, and fry in sizzling-hot olive oil until browned on both sides. Serve at once.

ZARZUELA
(*ASSORTED FISH IN PEPPERY SAUCE*)

The following recipe is a Catalan version of Zarzuela from Restaurante Pi in Vendrell (Tarragona). The Basques also make Zarzuela, but use cognac instead of absinthe and cayenne instead of ground white pepper. Either version requires five or more varieties of fish and shellfish. The dish is only good prepared and served at once, but it can be made in 20 minutes, start to finish.

SERVINGS: 6

6 *crayfish*
12 *prawns*
30 *mussels, cleaned*
6 *small squid, cleaned*
12 *center slices of two kinds of firm white fish (halibut, had-dock, sea bass)*
½ *cup olive oil*
1 *medium onion, minced*
¾ *cup canned tomato, mixed in an electric blender or forced through a sieve*

4 *dozen peeled, toasted hazelnuts*
3 *small cloves garlic, peeled*
3 *sprigs of parsley*
10 *drops of absinthe (substitute an anise-flavored liqueur such as anisette or a pinch of aniseed)*
1½–2½ *cups of water*
½ *tsp ground white pepper (or more if you like food pep-pery)*

salt to taste

Cut squid in rings. Open mussels by shaking them in a pan over moderate heat. Strain juice through a kitchen towel for use in sauce. Wash crayfish and prawns, but do not peel.

Brown onions slowly in olive oil. Increase heat, add tomato, and let it cook 1 minute. Season with pepper. Add slices of fish with squid cut in rings. Spoon sauce over them and let them cook over a rather hot fire. In a mortar, crush the hazelnuts with the garlic and parsley to a smooth paste (or mix in an electric blender with ½ cup water). When the fish has been cooking 4–5 minutes, turn it over. Season with salt. Two minutes later, add the strained juice

141

from the mussels, 1 cup cold water, and the prawns and crayfish. Cook 2 minutes more. Add cooked mussels. Dilute contents of mortar with ½ cup water. Add to sauce in pan and stir. Add water if necessary to prevent sauce from sticking to bottom of pan. When the slices of fish are tender, remove them to a warmed serving dish. Sprinkle liqueur over the sauce, stir it well over heat, and pour the contents over the fish in the serving dish.

CHAPTER 10

FOWL AND GAME

QUANTITIES of game are sold in Spanish shops and markets. In Madrid, partridge is as available and as economical as chicken, and quail, woodcock, pheasant, young pigeon, and wild hare are frequently found in stores and on menus.

Almost any bird is apt to find its way into the kitchen. Nets are set in the fields in the fall and spring to catch hundreds of small birds at a time, all of which are painstakingly plucked and cooked with rice or grilled or fried. The excuse that the birds eat the fall olive crop or the spring seed planting is secondary; the primary interest is in eating the birds. At the risk of protest from wildlife protection societies, I confess that when a platter of tiny fried birds was put before me, I not only ate them, I found them delicious, bones and all.

Among the domestic fowl, chicken is the most popular,

with duck following closely. The Spanish duck is quite large and looks like a cross between a goose and a duck. It is tender and not fat, as American ducks tend to be. Some of the partridge recipes given in this chapter can be made with chicken, as can all of the recipes for rabbit.

GALLINA CON SALSA DE ALMENDRAS
(*STEWING CHICKEN IN ALMOND SAUCE*)

SERVINGS: 6

1 large stewing chicken cut into small serving pieces

1 medium onion, chopped

2 cloves garlic, whole

12 peeled, toasted almonds

1 TB flour for sauce plus flour for dusting chicken

1 cup dry white wine

2 TB dark rum

*a small pinch of saffron, toasted and crushed ***

4 TB olive oil

salt and pepper to taste

Cut chicken into small serving pieces, dry thoroughly, dip in flour, sprinkle with salt and pepper, and fry slowly in hot olive oil with onion and peeled, whole garlic cloves. Bring water to boil on the side.

When chicken is nicely browned, remove chicken and garlic cloves. Stir in saffron and 1 TB flour. One minute later, add white wine and rum. When wine has reduced to half on fairly fast boil, replace chicken. Pour in enough boiling water to cover. Stir, add salt and pepper if necessary, and simmer, covered, until meat is tender. (Stewing chicken will take 1½–2½ hours.)

* To toast saffron, fold grains in a piece of paper, place paper on hot plate or any hot surface until paper begins to brown. Crush with pestle in mortar or bowl.

Crush garlic cloves in mortar with almonds. Dilute with a little of the chicken sauce, then stir it into the sauce in the casserole. Cook 5 minutes longer and serve.

NOTE: This recipe can be made with two or three tender chickens instead of a stewing chicken. If sauce seems too thin when cooking of chicken is almost completed, remove lid for remainder of cooking time.

GALLINA EN PEPITORIA (I)
(CHICKEN IN SAFFRON AND GARLIC SAUCE)
SERVINGS: 6

1 large stewing chicken cut in rather small serving pieces	4–5 TB olive oil center of a slice of white bread
1 medium onion, chopped fine	a pinch of saffron, toasted *
2 cloves garlic, minced	2 TB pine nuts
1 chicken liver	2 sprigs of parsley, chopped
yolks of 2 hard-boiled eggs	salt and pepper to taste

Heat 2–3 TB olive oil in a casserole. When oil begins to smoke, fry chicken, carefully dried, with onion and garlic. On the side, put to boil enough water to cover chicken.

In a skillet, fry pine nuts in 2 TB olive oil. Remove them to mortar. Fry bread and chicken liver (cover pan until liquid has cooked out of liver in order to avoid spattering grease). Remove bread and chicken liver to mortar. Mash them to a fine paste with parsley, yolks of

* To toast saffron, fold grains in a piece of paper, place paper on hot plate or any hot surface until paper begins to brown. Crush with pestle in mortar or bowl.

hard-boiled eggs, and toasted saffron. Dilute with a little boiling water.

When chicken is golden but not brown, sprinkle it with salt and pepper, pour mixture from mortar over it, and add boiling water to cover. Stir. Cook slowly, covered, until chicken is almost tender, then remove lid to allow sauce to thicken. To serve, strain sauce over chicken in serving dish.

NOTE: Stewing chicken will take 1½–2½ hours. The recipe can be made with young chickens, which may be tender in just 30 minutes. If sauce is too thin when chicken is done, remove chicken, boil sauce down, then reheat chicken in sauce.

GALLINA EN PEPITORIA (II)
(CHICKEN IN SAFFRON AND GARLIC SAUCE)
SERVINGS: 6

1 large stewing chicken cut in small serving pieces	*a pinch of saffron, toasted **
1 medium onion, chopped fine	*1 cup dry white wine*
	1 bay leaf
1 clove garlic, minced	*1 branch thyme*
2 raw egg yolks	*1 bunch parsley*
1 TB flour plus flour for dusting chicken	*5 TB olive oil*
	salt and pepper to taste

Dredge chicken in flour and brown with chopped onion in hot olive oil. Add minced garlic when onion is brown.

* To toast saffron, fold grains in a piece of paper, place paper on hot plate or any hot surface until paper begins to brown. Crush with pestle in mortar or bowl.

146

Sprinkle with 1 TB flour and toasted saffron. Brown flour, stirring to prevent burning. Salt and pepper lightly. Add white wine and let liquid reduce to half. Put in bay leaf, thyme, and parsley, all tied together. Pour in boiling water to barely cover fowl. Cook slowly with lid until tender. If sauce is not thick enough when chicken is almost done, finish cooking with lid off; if necessary, put sauce in separate pan and boil it down.

Just before serving, transfer chicken to warmed serving platter, strain sauce slowly into lightly beaten egg yolk while stirring constantly and vigorously. Pour over chicken and serve at once.

NOTE: Like the preceding recipe, this can be made with two or three young chickens instead of a large stewing chicken. The cooking time is then reduced from 1½–2½ hours to ½–¾ hour.

POLLO A LA CHILINDRÓN
(CHICKEN WITH PEPPERS AND TOMATOES)

Use two or three very young chickens cut in serving pieces instead of lamb in Cordero a la Chilindrón (p. 166).

POLLO EN ESCABECHE
(MARINATED CHICKEN)

This excellent dish, whose recipe was provided by the owner of the Restaurant Gayango in Madrid, was adapted by him from the marinade hunters use to preserve partridge when many are bagged at once. A most convenient pre-prepared dish to have on hand for a hot day, it will keep for days or weeks.

147

SERVINGS: 4

1 3-lb. chicken
1/4 cup olive oil
2 whole, peeled garlic
  cloves
1 lemon

1/2 orange
10 whole pepper grains
2 bay leaves
1/2 cup vinegar
2 cups dry white wine
salt to taste

Wipe chicken thoroughly. Heat olive oil and slowly brown chicken in a deep earthenware casserole. Fry chicken only until golden and do not allow it to form a crust. Pour over the fried chicken the following marinade: wine, vinegar, bay leaves, garlic cloves, pepper grains, lemon and orange, sliced, peel and all, and salt to taste.

Simmer chicken in marinade for 1 hour or until joints move easily. Keep covered with liquid at all times, adding wine and vinegar in the same proportions (4 to 1) as needed. When cooked, store chicken covered with marinade in an earthenware container in a cool place. Serve cold in sauce, surrounded by fluted slices of fresh orange and lemon.

CONEJO A LA JUANA
(RABBIT IN ALMOND SAUCE)

SERVINGS: 6

2 rabbits, 1 1/2–2 lbs.
  each, dressed and cut
  in serving pieces
2 medium tomatoes
1 1/2 heads garlic
1 medium-small onion
1/4 cup olive oil
salt to taste

15 peeled, toasted al-
  monds
3 cups hot water
1/4 cup cognac
a small pinch of cin-
  namon
2 cloves
2 graham crackers

148

Have rabbit livers put aside when rabbits are cleaned and quartered. Wash and dry rabbits, cut in serving pieces, and brown well in hot olive oil in casserole. Add an unpeeled tomato, half a head of garlic (peel, skin, and all), a sliced onion, ¼ cup cognac, cinnamon, and cloves.

While rabbits cook, grill or bake in oven a tomato and the whole head of garlic. Heat 3 cups water on the side. In a mortar, pound almonds. Add rabbit livers and crush them with almonds and the tomato peel and onion slices from the casserole. Fill mortar with hot water, mix, and add to casserole when rabbits begin to stick to pan.

Pound the fried or grilled tomato and the whole head of garlic in the mortar, dilute with hot water, and add to rabbits. Pour in enough additional hot water to cover rabbits and continue cooking until they are tender (about ¾ hour). Salt to taste.

Before serving, strain sauce through sieve and thicken it with two graham crackers pounded in a mortar with a bit of the sauce from the rabbits. Serve rabbits covered with sauce.

CONEJO CON CIRUELAS Y PIÑONES
(RABBIT WITH PRUNES AND PINE NUTS)

SERVINGS: 6

2 rabbits, 1½–2 lbs. each, dressed and cut in serving pieces	½ cup olive oil
	30 peeled, toasted almonds
4 medium tomatoes, peeled and chopped	a few sprigs of parsley
	tip of a bay leaf
2 cloves garlic, peeled	⅓ cup pine nuts (optional)
2 medium onions, chopped	20 dried prunes
salt to taste	

149

Heat olive oil in a casserole. Fry onions slowly until golden; add tomatoes and tip of bay leaf; continue frying.

Wash and dry rabbits; cut in serving pieces. When onion-tomato mixture has thickened, add rabbit and simmer, covered, for ½–¾ hour.

Crush garlic, almonds, and parsley in mortar; mix in ½ cup water. (This can be done in one step in an electric blender.) Add ground mixture to rabbit sauce, salt to taste, and cook additional ½ hour or until tender. While completing the cooking, simmer pine nuts and prunes in water in separate saucepans. The former will require 10–15 minutes; the cooking time of the dried prunes varies with the brand. Drain and add prunes and pine nuts to rabbit just before serving. (If added earlier, the pine nuts will not remain white and the prunes will over-sweeten the sauce.)

NOTE: Chicken or duck can be prepared in the same way.

PERDIZ CON CROQUETAS DE COL
(*PARTRIDGE WITH CABBAGE CROQUETTES*)

SERVINGS: 4

2 *tender, young par-*
tridges, cleaned and
dressed

2 *cloves garlic, peeled*

1 *onion*

1 *tomato*

½ *cup dry white wine*

⅓ *cup water (or meat*
stock or beef bouil-
lon)

tip of a bay leaf

a pinch of ground cin-
namon

1 *large cabbage*

1 *beaten egg*

flour for dusting

⅓ *cup olive oil for fry-*
ing

salt and pepper to taste

150

Preheat oven to 400°. Wash and dry partridges, rub with olive oil, salt, and pepper, and put them in a lightly greased oven pan with the onion, tomato, and garlic, all whole. After 20–25 minutes (or when the partridge is half roasted), pour in wine. When wine has almost entirely evaporated, add water or stock, bay leaf, and cinnamon. Baste partridge frequently during second half of roasting. Add a little more stock or water if necessary; there should be juice in quantity.

While partridge roasts, separate cabbage leaves. Boil the leaves whole in salt water until just tender, but not soft. Drain and rinse in cold water. To make the croquettes, take two or three leaves, fold in the tenderest part of the leaf, and roll up the croquette, giving it a round or oblong shape as you choose. Dust each croquette in flour, dip it in beaten egg, and fry it in hot olive oil until browned on all sides.

Fifteen minutes before the partridge is done, add the croquettes to the partridge sauce. To serve, cut each partridge in two, strain the sauce over the birds, and arrange the cabbage croquettes around them.

PERDIZ A LA VINAGRETA
(PARTRIDGE IN VINEGAR SAUCE)

SERVINGS: 4

4 young, tender partridges	a head of garlic
2 carrots	¼ cup olive oil (approximate)
3 small tomatoes	2 tsp flour
2 medium onions	1 heaping TB butter
¼ cup cognac	2 TB vinegar
¼ cup dry white wine	16 small onions
10 peeled, toasted almonds	salt and pepper to taste

151

Preheat oven to 400°. Cook the small onions in boiling water until tender; strain and set aside. Toast a head of garlic on the end of a fork over a gas flame until well browned (or roast garlic in hot oven). Peel and mash garlic in mortar with peeled, toasted almonds. Stir in ½ tsp olive oil and 2 tsp flour.

Peel and slice carrots and onions. Wash inside cavity of partridges with vinegar mixed with water. Rub the whole, cleaned partridges with olive oil, salt, and pepper, and put them in a lightly greased oven pan with carrots, onions, and three small whole tomatoes. Roast in 400° oven for 20 minutes. Pour cognac and wine over birds and continue roasting until they are browned and tender (the joints should move easily). Total cooking time for young partridge is approximately 45 minutes, and the birds should be basted frequently throughout.

When partridges are roasted, remove them to an ovenproof serving dish. Strain cooking juices into a saucepan, add the garlic-almond paste, a heaping TB of butter, and the 2 TB of vinegar. Boil slowly for 6–7 minutes. Season with salt and pepper.

Brown the small, pre-boiled onions in 2 TB olive oil. Pour sauce over partridges, add browned onions, and reheat dish in oven for 10 minutes, basting the birds with the sauce.

NOTE: If small onions are not available, substitute canned artichoke hearts. Strain and fry in olive oil before adding.

This recipe can be used for game birds other than partridge, but is not suitable for domestic fowl, such as chicken.

CHAPTER II

MEAT

WHILE the Spanish have the advantage over us in the matter of fish, our meat is hard to surpass. There is scarcely any beef in Spain, and the veal is not much like ours. Because the animals are slaughtered either at the age of two years or when still suckling, only milk-fed veal and something which is neither beef nor veal are ordinarily available. Most of the fillets and roasts look like miniatures to an American.

Suckling animals are a much-appreciated delicacy. In addition to veal, you can eat suckling kid, suckling lamb, and suckling pig in Spain. The flocks of kid and lamb that feed on mountain rosemary and thyme have an extraordinary flavor, best appreciated when the meat is cooked very simply. Mutton roasted over a campfire of rosemary bushes is a memory not quickly faded.

153

RUSTIDO A LA CATALANA
(*CATALAN ROAST*)

SERVINGS: 4

1 2-lb. veal roast	a branch of thyme
2 TB lard	6 grains black pepper
¼ cup dark rum	2 cloves
¾ cup dry white wine	1 bay leaf
1 head garlic, unpeeled	salt and pepper to taste
½ cinnamon stick	

This delicious dish is quick to assemble and, once cooking, needs very little attention.

Heat lard. Brown thyme, bay leaf, cinnamon stick, pepper grains, head of garlic, and cloves in a deep casserole with the meat over a moderate fire. Turn meat frequently until well browned, then sprinkle with salt and pepper, pour wine and rum over it, cover casserole, and cook over fairly low flame for 2 hours or until meat is tender. If necessary, add small amounts of hot water during cooking.

Before serving, strain sauce. Slice meat and serve in sauce. Meat reheated slowly in sauce the following day is excellent.

TERNERA A LA CONDESITA
(*VEAL WITH SHERRY*)

SERVINGS: 6

12 thin slices veal (about 2 oz. each)	juice of ½ lemon
6 medium cloves garlic	3 TB sherry
2 doz. peeled toasted almonds	3 TB olive oil for marinade
1 egg	4 TB olive oil for frying
1¼–1½ cups meat stock or beef bouillon	flour for dusting meat
	salt and pepper to taste

154

Flatten meat slices. Trim off all fat and put meat to soak in marinade of lemon juice and 3 TB olive oil while you prepare sauce.

For sauce, crush almonds in mortar with a little of the sherry. Toast garlic cloves unpeeled over gas flame until outside is blackened, then peel and fry in 1 TB olive oil. (If you have no flame, roast garlic cloves in oven until soft.) Reserve the olive oil for frying meat; add fried garlic to almonds. Crush garlic to a paste; mix in remaining sherry and 1¼ cups stock or beef bouillon. Season to taste with salt and pepper.

Before frying veal slices, wipe them and dip first in beaten egg, then in flour. Add 3 TB olive oil to that used for frying garlic and heat it until it will sear the meat instantly. Fry veal slices, two or three at a time, putting them in an earthenware or heavy-bottomed casserole when well browned on both sides.

When all meat is browned, pour sauce over it, bring it to a boil, and let it simmer for 10 minutes or until sauce thickens a little. Add a little meat stock or beef bouillon to thin or augment sauce if necessary.

Ternera a la Condesita is excellent served surrounded by small slices of bread fried in olive oil which each person can put under his meat and sauce when serving himself.

NOTE: The garlic in this dish will go undetected by many because the manner in which it is precooked removes its pronounced taste while permitting it to enrich the sauce.

TERNERA CON GUISANTES
(VEAL WITH GREEN PEAS)

SERVINGS: 6

1 3-lb. veal roast	1 rounded TB butter
1 carrot, sliced	1 rounded TB flour
2 small tomatoes (or 1	1 branch fresh thyme
tsp tomato purée)	(or 1/3 tsp dried
1 head garlic, unpeeled	thyme)
1/4 cup cognac	1 bay leaf
3/4 cup dry white wine	1/2 stick cinnamon (or
1 cup stock or beef	1/8 tsp powdered cin-
bouillon	namon)
1 lb. green peas	6 black pepper grains
3 TB olive oil	salt to taste

Heat olive oil in a casserole. When oil is hot, put in thyme, bay leaf, garlic, cinnamon, pepper grains, carrot, and tomatoes (if you use purée, add it later with the wine). Brown meat well on all sides with the herbs and vegetables over a moderate flame. When meat is brown, add cognac, wine, and bouillon or stock. Salt to taste and simmer over low fire, covered, for about 2 hours or until meat is very tender. Turn meat from time to time while cooking. Add water in small amounts if sauce becomes scarce or dry. Before meat is done, boil peas in a small amount of water until just tender; drain and set aside.

When meat is tender, remove it and strain sauce. Melt butter, stir in flour, dilute with a little of sauce and add to body of sauce to thicken it. Cook over low fire, stirring frequently until it thickens.

Remove string from roast if it was tied, cut it in slices,

and reheat it in sauce with the cooked peas. Serve meat on platter with peas and sauce over it.

NOTE: This dish is excellent made the day before and slowly reheated. It can be varied by the substitution of another precooked vegetable for the peas—artichoke hearts, tiny onions, or lima beans, for example.

PERDICES DE CAPELLÁN
(*MOCK PARTRIDGES*)

SERVINGS: 6

12 *very thin slices veal (weighing under 2 oz. each)*
12 *very thin slices cured (but not salty) ham*
12 *slices salami* *
1 *large garlic clove*

1 TB *dried herbs (thyme, basil, tarragon, rosemary, or any combination you prefer)*
3 TB *olive oil*
½ *cup white wine*
flour for dusting meat
salt and pepper to taste

Flatten veal slices to make them as thin as possible. On each, put one slice of ham and one slice of sausage. Roll firmly, tucking in loose edges; tie with thread. Dust in flour and brown well in hot olive oil in a flat casserole large enough to hold all the pieces without crowding.

When meat is browned, add dried herbs, crushed garlic clove, and wine. Cover and cook slowly ½–¾ hour. During cooking, add small quantities of water from time to time as sauce thickens. Season with salt and pepper

* This recipe, which comes from the Balearic Islands, traditionally uses the local sausage, *sobrasada,* a reddish, pasty sausage of distinct flavor. The suggested salami substitute works well and is used in parts of Spain where *sobrasada* is not available.

when almost ready to serve. Remove thread from meat and serve in sauce, which should be fairly thick.

MOCK PARTRIDGES WITH BRUSSELS SPROUTS

With the addition of Brussels sprouts, mock partridges make an excellent one-dish meal. For six servings, boil 1½ pounds of cleaned Brussels sprouts in very little salted water until just tender. Take care not to overcook. Dip sprouts in egg and fry in ¼ cup hot olive oil. Add vegetables to mock partridges 5 minutes before serving. They will absorb sauce and contribute to its flavor.

ESTOFADO
(*BEEF STEW*)

SERVINGS: 4

2 *lbs. lean stewing beef, cut in 2″ cubes*
1 *medium onion, cut in large slices*
2 *garlic cloves, un- peeled*
1 *large ripe tomato, un- peeled*
⅓–½ *cup olive oil*

½ *cup dry white wine*
2 TB *cognac*
1 *heaping* TB *flour*
1 *cup boiling water*
½ *tsp paprika*
½ *bay leaf*
1 *sprig fresh thyme (or ½ tsp dried thyme)*
a pinch of cinnamon
salt to taste

Heat 3 TB olive oil over high heat in a heavy metal casserole. When oil is on verge of smoking, brown meat rapidly, 1 pound at a time. When browned, remove it to a bowl. (If you do not have a metal casserole, brown the meat in a frying pan; then continue, using earthenware casserole.)

Add olive oil if needed and allow it to heat before frying the onion and garlic until brown. Add tomato cut in eighths; fry until juice has evaporated. Add cognac and wine; continue cooking over high flame until liquid evaporates. Reduce flame, add salt, paprika, cinnamon, thyme, bay leaf, and flour. Stir vigorously until flour is browned. Put meat back in casserole. Add a cup of boiling water, mix, cover, and simmer for 2 hours or until meat is tender. If the sauce becomes too dry during cooking, add boiling water in small amounts. If the sauce is too thin when the meat is done, remove meat and boil sauce uncovered until thick enough. The consistency of the sauce will vary with the amount of juice released by the meat.

Before serving, place meat in a dish and strain sauce over it.

NOTE: Estofado is a convenient dish for the hostess-cook because it is particularly delicious if prepared several hours in advance and reheated just before being brought to the table.

ESTOFADO CON CIRUELAS Y PIÑONES
(BEEF STEW WITH PRUNES AND PINE NUTS)
SERVINGS: 4

1 Estofado recipe (p. 158)	½ lb. dried prunes
	½ cup pine nuts

Prepare estofado as directed in preceding recipe. A half hour before serving, put prunes to boil in enough water to cover. Remove and strain when tender. Fifteen minutes before serving, boil pine nuts in water to cover in a separate saucepan. Drain and add pine nuts and prunes to estofado.

The prunes are added only at the last moment to avoid oversweetening the sauce; the pine nuts are added just before serving in order to preserve their whiteness.

ESTOFADO CON PATATAS
(*BEEF STEW WITH POTATOES*)

SERVINGS: 4

1 Estofado recipe (p. 158)   *4–6 large potatoes*

Prepare estofado as directed in the basic recipe. A half hour before serving, boil or fry potatoes cut in eighths. Add to estofado just before bringing to the table. (If added earlier, the potatoes may crumble.)

LOMO DE CERDO A LA ARAGONESA
(*LOIN OF PORK WITH ONIONS AND WHITE WINE*)

SERVINGS: 6

6 large, thick (¾″) slices of pork tender- loin or 6 pork chops
4 TB olive oil for mari- nade
5 TB olive oil for frying
½ clove garlic
6 whole pepper grains
1 clove

2 medium onions, chopped
1 TB wine vinegar
2 TB dry white wine
flour for dusting meat
¼–½ cup meat stock or beef bouillon
a few grains of toasted saffron **

salt and pepper to taste

* To toast saffron, fold grains in a piece of paper, place paper on hot plate or any hot surface until paper begins to brown. Crush with pestle in mortar or bowl.

Marinate pork overnight in 4 TB olive oil mixed with ½ clove garlic, the pepper grains, and the clove, all crushed to a pulp in a mortar.

Chop onions and fry slowly in 2 TB olive oil in a casserole. While onions are frying, dip meat in flour and fry it in 3 TB very hot olive oil in a large pan. Brown well on both sides. When onions are soft and golden, pour in 1 TB vinegar and let boil until liquid has evaporated.

Add fried slices of meat to onions, pour heated stock or bouillon into frying pan to rinse out all meat juice, and pour the stock and meat juice over meat and onions. Add 2 TB dry white wine and enough stock or bouillon to just barely cover the meat. Mix a little of the juice with a few grains of toasted saffron and stir into casserole. Salt to taste and sprinkle with black pepper.

Cook uncovered at slow simmer for 20 minutes. As sauce thickens, it may stick to bottom of casserole; scrape bottom of pan with spatula or flat spoon from time to time to prevent burning. Serve in casserole.

COCHINILLO ASADO
(ROAST SUCKLING PIG)

One of the great specialties of Castile, and of Segovia in particular, is suckling pig roasted in bakers' ovens, which are heated with wood before the meat is put to roast slowly to a melting tenderness covered with a succulent brown crust. To demonstrate the tenderness of the suckling pig, it is carved with a plate instead of a knife in Segovia.

The most famous place for suckling pig in Madrid is

161

Sobrino de Botin, a restaurant founded in 1725, where the dish is prepared in the original oven. The following is Sobrino de Botin's recipe for roasting the pig.

SERVINGS: 5–6

1 3-week-old pig weigh-
ing, cleaned and
dressed, approxi-
mately 6½ lbs.

4–5 cloves of garlic,
chopped

2 medium onions,
chopped

a bunch of parsley,
chopped

a sprig of thyme (or ½
tsp powdered thyme)

1 bay leaf

½ cup dry white wine

½ cup water

½ lb. lard

salt and pepper

Put bay leaf, thyme, chopped garlic, onions, and parsley inside pig. Salt and pepper outside of pig and place it in an earthenware dish. Pour in wine and water in equal parts (approximately ½ cup each) until bottom of dish is covered. Put lard in dish and roast in preheated moderate oven (350°) for 1 hour. Turn pig over, pouring off liquid which has formed. Brush skin with olive oil and return to oven. Continue baking until skin is crusty and golden brown. Baste frequently.

PORK AND SAUSAGES WITH WHITE BEANS

The recipe for this hearty meal in one dish was provided by a Catalan chef, Señor José Marlés.

SERVINGS: 8

1¾ lbs. dry white beans,
  cooked according to
  basic recipe (p. 185)
4 lbs. lean pork cut in
  bite-size pieces
1 large onion, unpeeled,
  cut in eighths
6 small tomatoes, un-
  peeled
6 cloves garlic, un-
  peeled
1 chorizo (or pep-
  peroni) sausage,
  whole

1 cooked pork sausage,
  sliced
⅓ cup dark rum
¼ tsp cinnamon
1 bay leaf
a pinch of cayenne pep-
  per
3 TB olive oil for frying
¼ cup olive oil for
  sauce
3 TB butter (optional)
salt to taste

Heat 3 TB olive oil in a large skillet and brown pork.
When pork is well browned, fry onion, tomatoes, and
garlic for 15 minutes. Add rum and 1 cup water. Salt to
taste. When sauce boils again, add whole *chorizo*, bay leaf,
and cinnamon. After 15 minutes, remove *chorizo*, tomatoes, garlic cloves, and onions. Pour in enough water to
barely cover the meat and cook over moderate flame with
lid on until meat is tender. Add more water if sauce
becomes dry.

Peel *chorizo* and garlic. Put in electric blender with
tomatoes and onion, ¼ cup olive oil, and ¼ cup water.
Blend to fine purée. (If you do not have an electric
blender, use a mortar and pestle, crushing the solid
ingredients to a fine paste before adding liquid.) Add
cayenne pepper to sauce until it is as hot as you like it (the
sauce should be somewhat peppery). Season with salt and
pass through sieve.

When meat is tender, stir in butter if you are using it. Cook sliced pork sausage with meat just long enough to heat it through; remove slices. Fold in white beans with spatula carefully to avoid bruising; allow beans to heat, then serve in cooking dish with sliced pork sausage on top of beans and meat. Serve sauce apart.

BUTIFARRA CON JUDIAS
(SAUSAGE WITH WHITE BEANS)

This is a classic Catalan dish, often eaten as a light supper or a midmorning snack.

SERVINGS: 4

4 large or 8 medium pork sausages

2 cups precooked dried white beans (p. 185)

3 TB olive oil

Prick sausages with a needle so they will not burst. Grill under broiler or over charcoal. Fry precooked beans in 3 TB olive oil over fairly high heat until browned, turning them with a broad spatula to avoid bruising. It is essential to use olive oil, which imparts a special flavor and consistency to the beans. When the beans are fried, pour a thin stream of olive oil over them, arrange in a warmed serving platter, and serve with the sausage on top.

NOTE: Sausage and white beans can be prepared in another manner which gives them quite a different flavor: fry the sausage slowly in a skillet, then remove to brown the beans quickly in the sausage grease.

CORDERO ASADO A LA MANCHEGA
(*ROAST LAMB FROM LA MANCHA*)

SERVINGS: 6

1 4–5-lb. leg of lamb	*½ tsp dried thyme*
1 medium onion,	*¼ cup cognac*
minced	*3 TB olive oil*
3 medium cloves garlic,	*10 black pepper grains*
minced	*salt to taste*
1 large bunch fresh	*¼–¾ cup water*
parsley, chopped	

Preheat oven to 400°. Trim excess fat and any thick skin from the leg of lamb. Rub lamb with salt and brown it in an earthenware casserole (or Dutch oven) in 2 TB olive oil. When well browned on all sides (browning will take at least 20 minutes), put it fat side up in oven in a roasting pan or casserole. Pour ¼ cup water in pan to prevent burning of meat juices.

Discard grease from the casserole in which the lamb was browned. Add a fresh TB of olive oil, heat it, and fry the minced onion, garlic cloves, and parsley with the dried thyme and whole pepper grains until the onions and garlic are soft.

Baste roast from time to time, adding more water in small quantities as needed to prevent burning. When roast is half done, pour ¼ cup cognac over it and spread onion and herb mixture on top lamb. Continue basting and adding water as needed until lamb is well done but still firm enough to be carved. A 4–5-pound leg of lamb will take approximately 2 hours. Serve with sauce.

165

CORDERO A LA CHILINDRÓN
(*LAMB WITH PEPPERS AND TOMATOES*)

SERVINGS: 6

2 *lbs. boned lamb, cut from shoulder or leg*	6 *large fresh red peppers or a 14-oz. can of pimientos*
1 *large onion, chopped*	
2 *large cloves garlic*	3 *oz. cured ham*
1 *can tomatoes* (*8 oz.*)	2 TB *olive oil*
salt and pepper to taste	

If you use fresh peppers, put them to roast in a 350° oven. They should be tender in approximately 45 minutes (which is about when you will need them).

Cut lamb in bite-size pieces and fry in hot olive oil with peeled whole garlic cloves in a casserole. Sprinkle lamb with salt and pepper while frying.

When meat is browned, add ham cut in short strips and onion, chopped fine. When onion is tender, add tomatoes and roasted, seeded peppers (or canned pimiento) cut in strips. Continue frying slowly until lamb is tender. The time will vary according to the tenderness of the meat: allow 40–60 minutes. Add a little water if the meat sticks to the pan, but bear in mind that this is more of a fried dish than a stew and should not be liquid when finished.

NOTE: Chicken, rabbit and veal are also made *a la Chilindrón* in Aragon and Navarre, where this method of preparation is very popular. Use young, tender animals, cut in small serving pieces.

CORDERO COCHIFRITO
(SAUTÉ OF LAMB WITH GARLIC AND LEMON)
SERVINGS: 6

2 lbs. boned lamb cut from leg or shoulder	½ tsp paprika
2 medium onions, chopped	several sprigs parsley, chopped
4 cloves garlic, minced	juice of ½ lemon
salt and pepper to taste	3 TB olive oil

Cut lamb in bite-size pieces and brown in 3 TB hot olive oil. Remove and set aside. Over moderate fire, fry chopped onion until golden. Add minced garlic cloves, stir in paprika with pan off fire, replace meat, add lemon juice, sprinkle with ground black pepper and salt to taste. Continue frying until meat is tender. Two or three minutes before serving, add chopped parsley and fry it with the meat.

NOTE: This recipe is delicious with leftover lamb.

CHULETAS DE CORDERO A LA NAVARRA
(BAKED LAMB CHOPS WITH HAM, SAUSAGE, AND TOMATOES)
SERVINGS: 6

2–3 rib lamb chops per person depending on size of chops	4 large, very ripe tomatoes, peeled and chopped
¼ lb. cured ham, cubed	2 TB lard
12 very thin slices of chorizo (or pepperoni) sausage	2 TB olive oil
1 medium-large onion, chopped fine	a very small pinch of salt
	a little ground black pepper

Preheat oven to 350°. Fry chops in combined lard and olive oil. As chops are browned, put them in a large, ovenproof casserole. In the same lard and olive oil, fry cubed ham with chopped onion. When onion is soft and golden, add peeled, chopped tomatoes. Let mixture boil 1 minute, mix in a very small pinch of salt and a little ground black pepper, and spread mixture over chops. Place chops in oven and bake, covered, for 30 minutes. This much can be done hours in advance if you prefer.

Ten to 15 minutes before serving, place thin slices of sausage over meat and bake in top part of hot oven until sausage begins to melt. Serve in the casserole in which it baked.

CHULETAS DE CORDERO CON ALL-I-OLI
(*RIB LAMB CHOPS WITH ALL-I-OLI SAUCE*)

This very typical Catalan dish is suitable for backyard grilling and for picnics, provided you can keep the all-i-oli sauce cool. The chops, two or three per person, are grilled under the broiler or over charcoal until well done, and are eaten with All-i-oli (pp. 188–191).

CHULETAS DE CORDERO AL ROMESCO
(*RIB LAMB CHOPS WITH PEPPERY SAUCE*)

In this variation, the chops are basted with romesco sauce as they are grilled. The recipe for Romesco on page 193 makes enough for chops for six people.

CHAPTER 12

VEGETABLES

VEGETABLES normally are served as a separate course in Spain, often as a first course. Potatoes, particularly fried potatoes, may accompany a dish, a few artichokes may be cooked in a sauce or a grilled tomato served with a fillet of pork, but a portion of green vegetables is almost always presented by itself.

If boiled, it is combined with another vegetable. One of the most common combinations in Catalonia is potatoes and cabbage leaves, seasoned with olive oil and salt. Potatoes are also cooked with green beans and slices of onion, sometimes accompanied by All-i-oli (pp. 188–191). A lone vegetable is more likely to be fried in batter, cooked in tomato sauce, or fried with sausage meat or ham. Many Spanish vegetable recipes, particularly those for dry vegetables, contain enough meat to be the main course at lunch or supper.

169

STUFFED ARTICHOKES (I)

SERVINGS: 8

8 *small artichokes*	2 TB *chopped parsley*
½ *lb. veal or beef*	½ *tsp nutmeg*
1 *hard-boiled egg*	½ *cup dry bread*
½ *lemon*	*crumbs*
2 TB *olive oil*	*salt to taste*

Clean artichokes under cold running water. Remove coarse leaves at bottom of stem and cut off stem to make an even base. Cut off tops of artichokes and trim pointed tips of lower leaves. Rub leaves with lemon to prevent their turning dark. Cook artichokes in boiling water until tender (20–30 minutes). They are done when a leaf pulls off easily. Drain well by squeezing them and save cooking water. Remove tender leaves in center and scrape out and discard hairy part with a spoon.

Fry meat in olive oil. Put meat through meat grinder and add to it the hard-boiled egg and the tender part of the artichoke leaves you removed. Season with nutmeg, chopped parsley, and a little salt. Fill artichokes. (This much can be done in advance.)

Preheat oven to 400°. Put stuffed artichokes in oven-proof casserole in which they fit so tightly they cannot fall apart. Cover bottom of casserole with the water in which the artichokes cooked. Sprinkle tops with bread crumbs and bake in upper part of oven 20 minutes or until meat is cooked and top of artichokes browned.

STUFFED ARTICHOKES (II)

SERVINGS: 6

6 *small, very tender artichokes*	1 *small tomato, whole*
6 *oz. sausage meat*	1 *medium clove garlic*
3 *hard-boiled eggs*	3 *doz. toasted almonds*
1 *beaten egg*	5 TB *olive oil*
1 *medium onion, sliced*	1 *cup water*
	flour for dusting
	½ *lemon*

salt and pepper to taste

Clean artichokes under cold running water. Cut off stems, trim pointed leaves, cut tops level, remove coarse outer leaves. Rub leaves with lemon. Open center of artichokes by spreading leaves so that you have a cavity to fill. Unless the artichokes are very young, remove the hairy part with a spoon.

Fry sausage meat in 2 TB olive oil and mix with hard-boiled eggs. Season with salt and pepper and fill artichokes. Tie tops with string. In the oil in which the sausage fried, brown the sliced onion. Fry tomato until it becomes a paste. Pour in 1 cup water and cook over moderate fire 7–8 minutes. Pass tomato-onion sauce through sieve, forcing it with mortar pestle or back of wooden spoon. Return strained liquid to fire.

Dip artichokes in beaten egg, then in flour, and fry in 3 TB olive oil heated to smoking point. Fry tops first to secure stuffing, then turn frequently until well browned all over.

While artichokes brown, pound garlic and almonds in mortar and add to sauce. If any filling is left over, add it to sauce too. Pour a little water in sauce when it thickens after the addition of almonds. When artichokes are browned, stand them in the sauce in an ovenproof casserole in which they fit so tightly they cannot fall apart. (This much can be done in advance.)

Cook artichokes slowly on top stove until tender (about 1½ hours). Add water to sauce in small amounts if sauce becomes too thick.

FRIED ARTICHOKES

For this you need very small, young, tender artichokes, hard to find in the United States. If you find them, this is a delicious and simple way of preparing them.

2–3 baby artichokes per   flour for dusting
person   salt and pepper
4–5 TB *olive oil*

Clean artichokes under running water, slice off tops so that only 1 inch remains above heart of vegetable, trim stems, and remove any tough outer leaves. Cook in boiling, salted water until tender. Test by pulling off a leaf: when it comes off easily, the artichoke is done. Cut boiled artichokes in eighths after draining well. Roll them in flour seasoned with salt and pepper and fry them in very hot olive oil. Drain briefly on paper or in a sieve and serve immediately.

FRIED EGGPLANT

SERVINGS: 6

3–4 young eggplants, no more than 2" in diameter
1 beaten egg (optional)

flour for dusting
⅓ cup olive oil (or enough to keep pan covered to a depth of ¼" throughout frying)
2 tsp salt

Wash and dry eggplants, cut in fine, even slices, salt lightly, and leave in bowl for a few hours.

Before cooking, dry eggplant thoroughly with a cloth, dust lightly in flour (or first in flour, then in beaten egg), and fry in small batches in olive oil heated to the verge of smoking. Turn when brown on one side. Drain briefly on paper and serve at once. The slices should be toast-brown and crisp.

NOTE: Zucchini can be substituted for eggplant in the preceding recipe. Soaking in salt is not necessary. Four or five medium zucchini will serve six.

FRIED CAULIFLOWER

SERVINGS: 4

1 small head cauliflower, cleaned and divided into flowerlets
¾ cup dry bread crumbs

1 egg beaten with 1 TB milk
½ cup olive oil
salt to taste

173

Cook cauliflower in boiling salted water until tender (10–15 minutes). Drain, dip in bread crumbs, then in beaten egg, and again in bread crumbs. Fry until brown in ½ cup olive oil heated to the verge of smoking. Drain briefly on paper and serve.

COLIFLOR AL AJO ARRIERO
(CAULIFLOWER IN HOT VINEGAR DRESSING)
SERVINGS: 4

1 small head cauli- flower, washed and divided into flower- lets	*2 TB vinegar*
	2 TB of the water in which the cauliflower cooked
2 garlic cloves	*1 tsp paprika*
¼ cup olive oil	*salt to taste*

Boil cleaned head of cauliflower until tender (10–15 minutes). On the side, heat olive oil and fry garlic cloves until browned. Discard cloves, add paprika with pan off fire, stir in 2 TB vinegar and 2 TB of water from the cooking of the cauliflower. Heat sauce, season with salt and pepper, and pour over drained cauliflower. Cover and cook 10 minutes over very low heat.

COLIFLOR EN SALSA ROMESCO
(CAULIFLOWER IN PEPPERY SAUCE)
SERVINGS: 4

1 small head cauli- flower, washed and divided into flower- lets	*1 recipe of Romesco Sauce (p. 193)*

174

Boil cauliflower (10–15 minutes) or steam it (20 or more minutes). Prepare the Romesco Sauce while the cauliflower is cooking. When it is tender, drain thoroughly, put in a warmed bowl, pour sauce over, toss, and serve.

FRIED BRUSSELS SPROUTS

SERVINGS: 4

2 *lbs. cleaned Brussels sprouts*
¾ *cup dry bread crumbs*

1 *egg*
1 TB *milk*
½ *cup olive oil*
salt to taste

Cook sprouts until just tender in boiling salted water (10–15 minutes). Take care not to overcook; very tender sprouts may be done in less time. Drain, roll in bread crumbs, dip in beaten egg, and roll in bread crumbs again. Fry until brown in olive oil heated to the verge of smoking. Drain on paper and serve.

GREEN BEANS IN TOMATO SAUCE

SERVINGS: 4

2 *lbs. green beans, cooked*
2 *medium tomatoes, peeled and chopped*

1 *small onion, chopped*
1 *heaping* TB *parsley, chopped*
2 TB *olive oil*
salt and pepper to taste

Fry onion in 2 TB olive oil over moderate fire until onion is soft and yellow but not brown. Fry tomato until liquid evaporates and sauce thickens. Add salt and pepper to taste, parsley, and well-drained cooked beans. Cook 3–4 minutes longer, stirring occasionally.

175

FRIED BROAD BEANS

SERVINGS: 4

2 *cups shelled beans*	2 TB *butter*
(*broad beans or lima*	2 TB *water*
beans)	3 TB *olive oil*
	salt and pepper to taste

Heat olive oil with 2 TB water. Fry beans until tender. They will quickly absorb water and should be done in 10–15 minutes. Before serving, mix 2 TB butter and season to taste with salt and pepper.

HABAS A LA CATALANA
(*SMOTHERED BROAD BEANS WITH SAUSAGE*)

SERVINGS: 6

3 *lbs. fresh, shelled*	1 *tomato*
broad beans or lima	2 *garlic cloves, peeled*
beans	1 TB *crème de menthe*
5 *oz. lean bacon or pork*	(*or a sprig of fresh*
fat, cubed	*mint*)
4 *oz. loin of pork, cut in*	2 *sprigs of parsley*
bite-size pieces	¼ *stick of cinnamon*
12 *slices of cooked*	1 TB *olive oil*
pork sausage	⅔ *cup water*
1 *medium onion,*	*salt to taste*
chopped	

Heat olive oil and fry bacon or pork fat, loin of pork, and chopped onion with the whole tomato. After a few minutes, add whole garlic cloves. When the meat is browned and the onion golden, remove the tomato. Add

the crème de menthe (unless you are using fresh mint);
let it boil down. Add the water and the shelled beans. Tie
together the bay leaf, parsley, cinnamon stick, and, if you
are using it, the fresh mint, and place it in the casserole.
Cover and boil over moderate fire for 15–20 minutes or
until beans are very tender; shake casserole from time to
time while beans cook. Before serving, remove herbs and
garlic cloves. Heat sausage slices with some of the juice
from the beans in a separate saucepan. (If there is not
enough juice to permit this, simmer the sausages in salt
water.) When beans are cooked, salt to taste and serve
with sausages on top.

MUSHROOMS IN TOMATO SAUCE
SERVINGS: 6

1½ lbs. mushrooms	1 branch of celery
1 medium onion, chopped fine	3 TB olive oil
2 cloves garlic, minced	a pinch of cinnamon
2 medium tomatoes, peeled and chopped	salt and pepper to taste

Cut off base of mushroom stems, wash mushrooms
thoroughly in cold water, and drain them. Put them in
boiling salt water for a few minutes until they are almost
tender, then rinse in cold water.

Heat olive oil; fry chopped onion with whole celery
until onion takes on color. Add garlic. When garlic takes
on color, add peeled, chopped tomato. Remove celery.
Season sauce with ground pepper and a pinch of cinnamon. Slice mushrooms, add them to sauce, salt to taste,
and boil gently for 15 minutes.

PATATAS EN SALSA VERDE
(*POTATOES IN SAUCE WITH PARSLEY AND PEAS*)

SERVINGS: 4

3 TB *olive oil*	3 *heaping* TB *chopped*
5 *medium potatoes*	*parsley*
3 *garlic cloves*	*hot water to cover*
4 TB *cooked, canned, or*	*salt and pepper to taste*
frozen peas	

Crush garlic cloves and mince. Fry slowly until golden in 3 TB olive oil in a flat earthenware casserole. Slice potatoes thin (but not paper thin). Have oil at barely sizzling temperature when potatoes are added. Spread them evenly over bottom of casserole and shake casserole to blend. One minute later, add 2–3 TB of water. Keep cooking over moderate heat and move casserole from time to time. Bit by bit, add hot water to cover the potatoes, always shaking the casserole to blend in the water. When the potatoes are covered and the sauce is fairly thick, add peas, season to taste with salt and pepper, give the casserole a swirl to mix, and put a lid over it. Cook covered until potatoes are tender. From time to time, remove lid and shake casserole to blend sauce and keep potatoes from sticking to the bottom. Just before serving, sprinkle with chopped parsley and shake casserole to mix parsley with sauce.

SPINACH WITH HAM

SERVINGS: 4

2 *cups cooked spinach*	3 *slices cured ham*
(2 *lbs. fresh or 2*	1 *garlic clove, peeled*
packages frozen)	¼ *cup olive oil*
salt (if necessary)	

Drain spinach well and chop coarsely. Heat ¼ cup olive oil and fry garlic clove until golden. Remove and discard clove. In the same oil, fry the ham cut into small pieces. When ham is lightly browned, add spinach. Toss continually while frying for 1–2 minutes and serve.

SPINACH WITH RAISINS AND PINE NUTS
SERVINGS: 4

2 *cups cooked spinach*	½ *cup seedless raisins*
(2 *lbs. fresh or 2*	¼ *cup pine nuts*
packages frozen)	2 TB *olive oil*
salt and pepper to taste	

Drain cooked spinach thoroughly and chop coarsely. Heat olive oil in skillet. Fry raisins and pine nuts until the latter are golden. Add spinach, season with salt and pepper, toss constantly while frying for 2 minutes, then serve.

PISTO

Pisto, which resembles the *pipérade* of the French Basques, is made throughout central and northwestern Spain in ways varying from region to region. Sometimes the *pisto* contains only vegetables; sometimes eggs are scrambled with the vegetables or poached on top. Two versions follow, one from La Mancha, one from the Rioja.

PISTO MANCHEGO
(PISTO LA MANCHA STYLE)

SERVINGS: 6

2 *very thick slices of cured ham*	1 *large (14-oz.) can of pimiento or 2 large, seeded red peppers*
2 *large ripe tomatoes, peeled and chopped*	3 TB *butter*
2 *medium onions, thinly sliced*	1 TB *olive oil*
10 *eggs*	*salt and pepper to taste*

Dice ham and fry in butter and olive oil in a fairly large casserole, preferably earthenware. Remove ham and fry sliced onions until soft but not browned. Add chopped tomatoes. Return ham to casserole. Add pimiento or fresh peppers cut in fine strips. Sprinkle with black pepper, cover, and cook over low fire until mushy. This much can be prepared in advance.

Just before serving, beat eggs with salt and pepper and mix into vegetables over a very low fire while turning casserole and scraping the bottom of it to keep the eggs from sticking. Serve when eggs are still moist.

NOTE: Other vegetables can be introduced into the *pisto* at will. For example, a cup of lima beans, broad beans, or string beans might be fried with the ham. If you add a vegetable, reduce the quantity of pimiento.

PISTO A LA RIOJANA
(PISTO RIOJA STYLE)

SERVINGS: 6

3 large tomatoes	1 medium green pepper
2 medium eggplants	2 whole, peeled garlic
2 medium red peppers	cloves
2 medium onions,	3 TB olive oil
chopped fine	salt and pepper to taste

Fry the chopped onions with the garlic cloves in olive oil. When the onions are soft (but not browned), add peppers, peeled, seeded, and cut in thin slices. Five minutes later, add tomatoes, peeled and chopped, with eggplants, diced, but not peeled. Season with salt and pepper and cook, covered, on slow flame until peppers are very tender. Good reheated.

MENESTRA DE LEGUMBRES
(BRAISED SPRING VEGETABLES)

The menestra, a favorite Basque dish, is made only when the spring vegetables are young and tender: in April, May, and June. The following recipe is from Casa Nicolasa in San Sebastián. The peas, whose pods are only 1½ inches long, must come from a certain strip of land on one specific mountain behind the town; the broad beans are the size of a shirt button, and the potatoes measure 1 inch in diameter at most. Pounds and pounds of the tiny fresh vegetables are shelled and peeled for each portion.

181

SERVINGS: 4

1 cup shelled baby broad beans	*3–4 cups meat stock or beef bouillon*
2 cups shelled spring peas	*2 thick slices lean bacon or salt pork, cubed*
12 pea pods	
16 tiny new potatoes	*1 thick slice cured ham*
4 young artichokes	*4 thin slices cured ham*
12 white asparagus tips	*1 rounded* TB *butter*
2 leaves tender lettuce, chopped fine	*7* TB *olive oil*
	1 rounded TB *flour*
1 small onion, minced	*flour for dusting*
1 medium onion, sliced thin	*1 beaten egg*
	1 lemon
salt to taste	*½ tsp sugar*

OPTIONAL:
1 poached egg per person
For poaching:
boiling salted water
1 TB *vinegar*

Broad beans: In a large saucepan, slowly fry one thick slice of lean bacon or salt pork cut into cubes in 1 TB olive oil. When the bacon has become soft, add a small minced onion. After the onion takes on color, put in a cup of shelled broad beans with ½ tsp sugar and two leaves of chopped lettuce. Let the beans fry for 1–2 minutes. Pour in 3 cups of meat stock or bouillon and cook beans at a slow boil for 2 hours uncovered. Add meat stock or bouillon as liquid evaporates. Season with salt when almost cooked.

Peas and potatoes: Break the ends off a dozen pea pods

and put them to boil in 6 cups of water. Heat 2 TB olive
oil in a small skillet. Slowly fry a thick slice of lean bacon
or salt pork cut in cubes. When it has browned a little, put
in a thinly sliced medium onion. Stir and shake the pan
while the onion fries until soft and golden, but not brown.
Pour off excess grease before adding 1 rounded TB flour.
Immediately pour contents of skillet into water in which
pea shells are boiling. Boil together for 30 minutes. Force
through a sieve into another saucepan. Add shelled peas
and peeled new potatoes. Bring to a boil and simmer for 2
hours. After 1 hour, add to the peas and potatoes a cubed
slice of cured ham fried for 2–3 minutes in 1 rounded TB
butter. Add a little meat stock or bouillon as liquid in
which peas and potatoes are cooking evaporates.

Asparagus: Scrape off tough outer fibers, cut off thick
part of stalk, and cook until tender in boiling salted water.
If prepared in advance, keep in its own cooking liquid;
reheat in the same liquid before serving.

Artichokes: Peel off all coarse exterior leaves until only
the tender center part remains. Cut choke to a maximum
height of 2 inches. Clean in cold water, rub with half a
lemon, and cook in boiling salted water to which you have
added the juice of half a lemon and the two squeezed
lemon halves. Cook until the leaves can be pulled off
easily. If prepared in advance, keep in its own cooking
liquid. Before serving, cut each artichoke in eight parts,
dip in flour, then in beaten egg, and fry in 4 TB hot olive
oil.

To serve: Place a portion of each vegetable on each
plate. Fry one piece of cured ham per person and serve it
on top of the broad beans. If you wish to have the
menestra with egg, poach one egg per person in boiling
salted water to which you have added 1 TB vinegar. Break

each egg into a saucer and slide it into the boiling water. Scoop eggs out 4 minutes later and immediately place them in a pan of cold water. Trim the ragged edges with a knife or kitchen shears. Serve the egg on top of the peas and potatoes.

BOILED RICE

Plain boiled rice is traditionally served with Shangurro (pp. 123–124) and Chicken en Pepitoria (pp. 145–146). It can be cooked in advance and heated shortly before serving.

SERVINGS: 6

2 *cups raw rice*	*1 large potful of boiling*
juice of ½ lemon	*water*
3–4 TB *butter*	*1 tsp salt*

Add lemon juice and salt to boiling water. When it is boiling rapidly, toss in rice and boil uncovered over a hot fire 15–20 minutes or until done. The cooking time for rices varies. Test frequently.

When rice is cooked, pour off boiling water and leave pot under running cold water for 10–15 minutes. Strain. Leave rice in colander or strainer until it is to be used. A few minutes before serving, spread rice over bottom of baking dish, dot lightly with butter, and warm in moderately hot oven. Press warm rice in a cup, leave it there a moment, then unmold on serving platter.

BASIC RECIPE FOR COOKING CHICK-PEAS

SERVINGS: 4

2 *cups dried chick-peas*	*1 tsp baking soda*
1 onion, sliced	*½ tsp salt*
1 garlic clove, peeled	

184

Wash chick-peas, sort over to eliminate any stones and bits of shell, and soak overnight before using. Put in casserole with salt, soda, sliced onion, and peeled garlic clove. Cover with tepid water 4 fingers higher than the level of the chick-peas. Cook uncovered over low fire until tender (but not mushy). Chick-peas should boil gently throughout cooking time, which will be between 3 and 6 hours. They must be covered with water at all times. If it is necessary to add, use boiling water. When cooked, drain thoroughly and remove onion and garlic.

NOTE: Cooked chick-peas are good in omelets (see p. 86). They are sometimes served alone, fried in olive oil, and sometimes sautéed with cooked spinach or a little minced garlic and ham.

BASIC RECIPE FOR COOKING DRIED WHITE BEANS

SERVINGS: 4

2 *cups dried white beans*
1 *onion*
1 *carrot*
a sprig of thyme or other fresh herb

1 *clove garlic, peeled*
1 *bay leaf*
2 *cloves*
salt to taste

Sort out any damaged beans or bits of stone. Do not presoak. Wash under running water and place in casserole with onion stuck with cloves, carrot, bay leaf, garlic clove, and sprig of thyme. Cover with tepid water to a level 3 fingers above surface of beans. Cook with lid on over very low fire until beans are tender, but not mushy or easily bruised. Drain thoroughly and discard vegetables and spices with which beans cooked. Salt beans only when cooked.

Beans should be from current year if possible. Unless they have been subjected to special processing, they will need to cook 1½–3 hours.

NOTE: Cooked white beans are served with tomato-onion sauce (p. 193), used in omelets (p. 85), or fried to accompany meat or sausage (p. 164).

WHITE BEANS WITH CHORIZO

SERVINGS: 6

1 lb. dried white beans	2 chorizo (*or pepperoni*) *sausages*
1 small onion	
3 medium cloves garlic	3 TB *olive oil*
1 TB *flour*	*1 bay leaf*

salt and pepper to taste

Put bay leaf, peeled garlic cloves, and half the onion in a pot with the white beans. Pour in cold water until it reaches 2 inches above the beans. Bring to a boil over slow fire with lid, then remove lid and simmer until beans are tender (1½–3 hours).

When beans are almost tender, remove onion, garlic cloves, and bay leaf. Chop second half of onion. Fry it in 3 TB olive oil and either mash it in a mortar or force it through a sieve. In the same oil, brown the flour. Add a little of the liquid from the cooking of the beans, mix well, and add to bean pot with onion purée. Add the *chorizo* sausages, whole, and boil them gently with the beans for 10 minutes. Serve drained beans with *chorizo* sliced on top.

PRESERVED MUSHROOMS

Home-preserved mushrooms have much more flavor than most canned varieties and preserving is a very simple process.

Prepare salt brine by boiling salt with water for 20 minutes in the proportions of 1 cup salt to 4 cups water.

Let brine cool while you clean mushrooms well, cut off tough ends of stems, and peel stems if skin is thick. Cook mushrooms in boiling water for 3 minutes, rinse in cold running water, drain, and pack in glass jars. Pour cooled brine in jars to fill to the neck. Top with a thin layer of olive oil to seal out air. Store covered lightly with a piece of paper to keep out dust.

Before using preserved mushrooms, desalt by soaking in several changes of water for half a day, then cooking in boiling water for 5 minutes and rinsing in cold water.

CHAPTER 13

———◆———

SAUCES

ALL-I-OLI (GARLIC MAYONNAISE)

RECIPES for all-i-oli date back to the tenth century, and
the sauce is much older than that. According to the
gastronomic authority Dionisio Perez,* it probably originated in Egypt and was introduced to Spain and France by
the Romans. Its name comes directly from the Latin for
garlic (*allium*) and oil (*oleum*). The classic Catalan all-i-
oli, used on fish, meat, vegetables, and salads, is made
without egg yolks. This requires the use of many raw
garlic cloves—too many for all but true garlic enthusiasts.
For the latter, a classic Catalan recipe has been included.
Outside Catalonia, the sauce (which is known as *ajolio* in
Aragon and *ajiaceite* in Andalusia) always includes egg
yolk.

* Enrique Sordo, *Arte Español de la Comida,* Barcelona: Editorial Barna, S.A., 1960.

188

All-i-oli is easy to make providing certain rules are observed, rules equally applicable to mayonnaise. The ingredients, particularly the olive oil, must be at room temperature. The oil must be added very gradually and the sauce must be stirred constantly and in the same direction all the while. Should the sauce "turn" or separate, put an egg yolk in a bowl and gradually add the curdled sauce to it while stirring constantly and in the same direction. All-i-oli will keep several days under refrigeration.

CLASSIC CATALAN ALL-I-OLI

SERVINGS: 1 cup of sauce

½ large head of garlic, peeled
½ tsp lemon juice or wine vinegar
1 cup olive oil at room temperature
a pinch of salt

Mash garlic to a smooth paste in mortar. Stirring constantly in the same direction, add olive oil very gradually. When mixture is as thick as a good mayonnaise, add lemon juice or vinegar. Still stirring, gradually add remaining olive oil. Salt to taste.

CATALAN ALL-I-OLI WITH BREAD

SERVINGS: 1 cup of sauce

5–6 garlic cloves, peeled
half the center of a slice of white bread
½ tsp lemon juice or wine vinegar
1 cup olive oil at room temperature
a pinch of salt

The addition of bread permits the use of less garlic. Mash bread and garlic in mortar together with salt.

189

Proceed according to directions for Classic Catalan All-i-oli.

ALL-I-OLI WITH EGG YOLKS

This and the following versions will be more appetizing to those who like garlic, but prefer it in moderation.

SERVINGS: 1½ cups of sauce

2 *cloves garlic, peeled*
1 TB *lemon juice or wine vinegar*
2 *egg yolks*

1½ *cups olive oil at room temperature*
a few drops of cold water

salt to taste

Put a few drops of cold water and a few drops of lemon juice or vinegar in a mortar with the garlic. Mash garlic well. Add raw egg yolks and blend. While stirring tirelessly in the same direction, add olive oil very gradually. Blend in additional lemon juice or vinegar. Salt to taste.

ALL-I-OLI WITH MUSTARD

SERVINGS: 1½ cups of sauce

1 *clove garlic, peeled*
1 *tsp lemon juice or wine vinegar*
2 *egg yolks*
1½ *cups olive oil at room temperature*

a few drops of cold water
1½ *tsp hot prepared mustard*
salt to taste

Put a few drops of cold water and a few drops of lemon juice or vinegar in a mortar with garlic. Mash garlic well. Add raw egg yolks and blend. Add olive oil very gradually

190

while stirring in the same direction. When all the olive oil has been absorbed, stir in mustard. Vary the amount of mustard according to the strength of the product and your own preference. Add salt if necessary.

ALL-I-OLI WITH TOMATOES

SERVINGS: 1¾ cups

3 *medium cloves gar-*
lic, peeled

2 *egg yolks*

1 *cup olive oil at room*
temperature

2 *large, ripe tomatoes,*
peeled and seeded

a generous pinch of salt

Prepare basic sauce by mashing garlic with salt in mortar, stirring in egg yolks, and very gradually adding olive oil while stirring in the same direction. Lastly mix in tomatoes, peeled, squeezed to eliminate seeds, and mashed to a pulp in a separate bowl.

Popular in Andalusia, this sauce is excellent with salads, cold fish, and cold meats.

SALSA MAHONESA
(*MAYONNAISE*)

The Spanish claim this as their own, with the city of Mahon on the Balearic Island of Menorca as its birthplace. The Duc de Richelieu is said to have introduced it to France, and the French promptly appropriated it. Some authorities argue that the original sauce from Mahon always contained some garlic and was actually not mayonnaise, but a light all-i-oli. Whether it was the French who first thought of omitting the garlic or not, the Spanish make mayonnaise without garlic as follows.

191

SERVINGS: 1½ cups of sauce

2 *egg yolks*
2 TB *lemon juice or*
wine vinegar
1½ *cups olive oil at*
room temperature

1 *tsp cold water*
½ *tsp salt*
a pinch of white pepper

In a mortar, mix egg yolks with a few drops of the lemon juice or vinegar. Very slowly add olive oil while stirring constantly. When sauce begins to thicken, blend in 1 tsp cold water. After all oil has been added, mix in salt, pepper, and the remaining lemon juice or vinegar.

If sauce should curdle, put an additional yolk in a bowl and pour curdled sauce into bowl in a very thin stream while stirring constantly.

SALSA COLORADA
(RED SAUCE)

Because the garlic is precooked, this sauce does not have a particularly strong garlic flavor, even though it calls for a head of garlic. It is particularly good with boiled vegetables, cold meats, and cold or hot fish.

SERVINGS: 1½ cups

3 *small tomatoes*
1 *head of garlic*
2 *yolks of hard-boiled*
eggs
12 *almonds, peeled and*
toasted

¾ *cup olive oil*
¼ *cup wine vinegar*
½ *hot chili pepper (or*
cayenne pepper to
taste)
salt to taste

Bake unpeeled tomatoes and garlic in oven until tomatoes are very soft. Remove peel from tomatoes and garlic, mash in mortar or electric blender with pepper. Add yolks of hard-boiled eggs with almonds; when well blended, gradually mix in oil and vinegar. Season with salt if necessary.

SALSA ROMESCO
(*ROMESCO SAUCE*)

Romesco is a specialty of the province of Tarragona, where contests are held in which over two dozen chefs may compete for the championship of Romesco making. The peppery sauce is used primarily with fish, but is good with vegetables and excellent for basting grilled mutton chops. The sauce can be made in an electric blender in less than 5 minutes and comes out very well, although chefs competing in the Romesco contest always use a mortar and pestle, which, they say, extract more oil from the nuts.

SERVINGS: 1–1½ cups of sauce

1 small tomato, peeled and seeded
1 small dried hot chili pepper (substitute powdered cayenne if chili peppers are not available)
3 cloves garlic, peeled
2 doz. hazelnuts, toasted and shelled
¾ cup olive oil
¼ cup wine vinegar
1 tsp salt

Grind nuts, pepper, tomatoes, and garlic in a mortar or an electric blender with salt; gradually add olive oil. When sauce thickens, blend in vinegar.

TOMATO-ONION SAUCE

SERVINGS: 3½–4 cups of sauce

6 very ripe, large tomatoes, peeled, seeded, and chopped (or 3–4 cups canned tomatoes)
2 large onions, chopped fine
½ cup olive oil
pepper and salt to taste

193

Heat oil to the verge of smoking in a large skillet. Fry onions until golden. Add tomatoes, season with salt and pepper, and cook slowly until all liquid has evaporated and sauce has thickened (10–15 minutes).

NOTE: If the ripe tomatoes are not sweet, add a pinch of sugar to the sauce. The sauce may be seasoned with garlic if you like: add a minced clove or two when onions are golden. Tomato-onion sauce is the base for countless recipes, and is used for foods of pronounced flavor such as mussels or cod, and for vegetables.

TOMATO-GARLIC SAUCE

SERVINGS: 3–3½ cups of sauce

6 *very ripe, large toma-* *toes, peeled, seeded,* *and chopped (or 3–4* *cups canned toma-* *toes)*	3–4 *large garlic cloves,* *minced* ⅓ *cup olive oil* *pepper and salt to taste*

Heat olive oil to the verge of smoking in a skillet. Fry the minced garlic cloves until browned. Add chopped, seeded tomatoes, season with salt and pepper, and cook until all liquid has evaporated and sauce has thickened.

NOTE: If tomatoes are not sweet, add a pinch of sugar to sauce.

PARSLEY SAUCE

½ *clove garlic*	2 TB *olive oil*
1 *boiled potato*	2 tsp *wine vinegar*
several sprigs of parsley	*several* TB *stock or beef*
salt and pepper to taste	*bouillon*

If you use an electric blender, mix all ingredients simultaneously. If you use a mortar, crush garlic, potato,

194

and parsley together. Blend in vinegar; gradually add olive oil, followed by as much bouillon or stock as needed to make the sauce the desired consistency. Season with salt and pepper to taste.

CHAPTER 14

DESSERTS

SPANISH desserts are usually simple: dried figs, cheese, almonds, and fresh fruit. Many of the more elaborate desserts served in Spain are French, although there are some excellent Spanish custards and creams, and the classic Riz à l'Impératrice is of Spanish origin. Rice pudding is often served at the family table; a bizcocho, or spongecake, will almost always be listed on a restaurant menu, and flan, a caramel custard, is probably the most common of all desserts. However, by the time you have gotten through the salad, fish, and meat courses of a Spanish meal, you are usually delighted to have only fruit, dried figs, or almonds for dessert. The almonds are sometimes accompanied by a slice of Gouda-type cheese; sometimes the figs are stuffed with toasted almonds, one to a fig, an easy but extraordinary combination.

The simplicity of the desserts on Spanish menus should not mislead anyone into thinking that the Spanish do not like sweets or do not know how to make them. Spanish pastries are excellent and consumed in quantities, but usually in the late afternoon, not at meals. Writing of her childhood in Seville, one Spanish cookbook author recalls seeing meringues the size of melons and layer cakes so large two men were needed to carry them.* Every province of Spain has its regional pastries, many so good and so distinctive that they should be classic recipes abroad as well as within Spain.

There is little use of butter or baking powder and a very heavy use of eggs, particularly egg yolks. Pastry doughs are often made with olive oil and even fried in it, but any mild-flavored cooking oil may be substituted. Pounded almonds serve as flavoring and also as a flour substitute in many cakes and cookies. Cinnamon is popular, particularly mixed with sugar and sprinkled on top of sweets; orange and lemon peel are used extensively, and anise is common in Andalusia, the Levante, and Catalonia. Because few private houses used to have ovens, many cookies and small tea cakes are fried. The scarcity of ovens probably accounts for the immense popularity of doughnuts, crullers, and fritters.

Spanish pastries and desserts use so many egg yolks that the disposal of the whites poses a problem for those too thrifty to throw them out. If covered, egg whites will keep in the refrigerator for days and in the freezer for much longer, but that only postpones the dilemma. The extra whites can be used instead of whole beaten egg for dipping fritters and croquettes prior to frying, and an extra egg white in an omelet will make it rise higher. Two to four surplus egg whites are called for in the recipes for Almendrados (pp. 214–215) and Orange Cream (p.

* Marquesa de Parabere, *Historia de la Gastronomía,* Madrid: Espasa-Calpe, S.A., 1943.

200). Aside from these suggestions, the solution is to be sought in non-Spanish dishes: standard American favorites using from two to twelve egg whites such as angelfood cake, white and silver cakes, macaroons, meringues, orange Bavarian cream, prune whip, meringue pies, chiffon pies, and a number of cooked cake icings.

FLAN
(CARAMEL CUSTARD)

Contrary to instructions for caramel custard in almost every cookbook, this recipe calls for a hot oven. Rather than glazing each mold with caramelized sugar, devote one small saucepan exclusively to the making of caramel. The pan need never be washed, and the molds will be much easier to prepare and to clean.

SERVINGS: 6 large or 12 small custards

⅔ *cup sugar for caramel*	1 *cinnamon stick cut in pieces*
1 *cup sugar for custard*	1 *tsp dried orange peel*
4 *cups milk*	*or a large peel from*
4 *eggs*	*fresh lemon or orange*

Preheat oven to 450°. Simmer milk slowly for 5–6 minutes with orange or lemon peel, cinnamon stick, and 1 cup sugar. In the meantime, prepare caramel by melting ⅔ cup sugar in a small pan. Watch constantly and move pan so that sugar will take on an even medium-brown color without burning. When sugar is brown, pour a little into each mold. Do not be concerned if caramel does not cover bottom of mold: it will spread over bottom during baking.

Let milk cool for a few minutes before straining into eggs stirred just enough to mix yolks and white thoroughly. Blend eggs and milk. Remove any foam that

198

accumulates: foam makes bubbles in custard.

Place filled molds in pan of cold water; water should cover bottom two-thirds of molds. Bake in 450° oven for 30–45 minutes or until done. Do not allow water to boil. Normally the custard will be done at about the time the water is on the verge of boiling. If water appears to be about to boil when custard is not yet baked, add cold water. Custard is done as soon as it is firm to the touch and slightly browned on top. Serve chilled. Unmold just before serving.

The flavoring of flan is limited only by the imagination. Flan will take on any seasoning or combination of seasonings you fancy: simply cook the flavoring ingredient in the milk until the milk has acquired the flavor. Some suggested variations follow.

ORANGE AND LEMON FLAN
Omit cinnamon stick. Add peel from half an orange and half a lemon.

VANILLA FLAN
Omit cinnamon. Add a vanilla bean broken in pieces or a teaspoon of vanilla extract.

RUM FLAN
Replace cinnamon and lemon or orange peel with 3 TB dark rum and half a vanilla bean broken in bits.

CREMA CATALANA
(CATALAN CREAM CUSTARD)
SERVINGS: 6

4½ cups milk	3 TB cornstarch
7 egg yolks	1 cinnamon stick
1⅓ cups sugar	rind of ½ lemon

Heat 3½ cups milk with cinnamon stick broken in pieces and lemon rind. Bring to a boil and simmer 5–6 minutes.

Separate yolks from whites. Add half of remaining cold milk to yolks and beat well. Add rest of cold milk to cornstarch and beat.

Strain boiled milk into clean saucepan. While stirring it constantly over the fire without letting it come to a boil, add in rapid succession ⅔ cup sugar, the egg yolk mixture, and the cornstarch diluted in milk. The custard will thicken quickly. Continue stirring until it is the consistency of a thick cream sauce. Pour at once into six shallow dessert plates.

When custard has cooled to room temperature, sprinkle surface with remaining sugar. Put under hot broiler just long enough to turn sugar an even light brown. Chill cream before serving.

NOTE: Catalan cream custard can be made with only five egg yolks, or, for a very rich dessert, with as many as ten yolks for 4½ cups of milk.

CREMA DE NARANJA
(ORANGE CREAM CUSTARD)

SERVINGS: 4

2 cups milk	6 egg whites
⅔ cup sugar	grated peel of 1 orange
2 egg yolks	peel of ½ orange

Beat milk, sugar, grated orange peel, egg yolks, and egg whites together until foamy and stiff. Strain into upper part of double boiler. Add peel of half an orange. Cook over hot but not boiling water for 20 minutes, stirring from time to time to prevent formation of lumps. In 20 minutes or when custard is as thick as a heavy cream sauce, pour into four individual dessert dishes. Chill before serving.

TOCINO DE CIELO
(RICH CUSTARD)

SERVINGS: 8–10

2¼ cups sugar	15 egg yolks
¾ cup plus 2 TB water	1 whole egg
peel of ¼ lemon	½ cup sugar for cara-melizing mold

Heat ½ cup sugar in a saucepan until it thickens and turns light brown. Line a 10-inch ring mold with the caramel.

Heat 2½ cups sugar with water and lemon peel in a saucepan over a slow fire. Simmer for approximately 30 minutes. Test frequently by dipping a tablespoon in the syrup and holding it vertically over the pan. Wait for the last drop: the syrup is done as soon as a thin, short thread forms at the end of the last drop.

Remove from fire and let cool to room temperature. In a large bowl, mix the yolks and the egg just enough to blend (do not beat). Continuing to stir the eggs, gradually pour in the cooled syrup. Strain the mixture. Put the caramelized mold on top of a plate in a pan of water which is hot but not boiling. (The purpose of the plate is to keep the mold from touching the hot bottom surface.) Add water to one-third the height of the mold. Pour in the custard, remove any foam, cover as hermetically as possible, and cook over a slow fire for about 1 hour. From time to time, remove lid to take off any foam that has formed. Serve unmolded and slightly chilled.

ARROZ CON LECHE
(*RICE PUDDING*)

SERVINGS: 4

1 cup rice	1 TB butter
5½ cups milk	a pinch of salt
1 rounded cup sugar	flavoring: 1 vanilla bean
powdered cinnamon for sprinkling	or 1 tsp vanilla extract

Scald rice as follows: bring to a boil several cups of water, toss in rice, and boil for 3 minutes while stirring. Drain and rinse under cold water.

Bring milk to a boil with vanilla. When milk is boiling, pour in scalded rice slowly so that boiling is not interrupted. Add butter, sugar, and salt. Let boil hard for 5 minutes, then cover and reduce flame to very low (or protect rice from burning by placing asbestos pad over moderate flame). Cook slowly, covered, until rice is done (about 1 hour). Check after 20 minutes to see whether more milk should be added; if rice is dry, add boiling milk. When pudding is cooked, rice grains should be soft but separate in a creamy thick sauce. Remove vanilla bean and pour pudding into serving dish to cool. When cool, powder with a little cinnamon.

NOTE: For variation, substitute a cinnamon stick and a small piece of orange peel for the vanilla. Tie the orange peel in cheesecloth and remove it when pudding is cooked.

ARROZ CON LECHE AL ESTILO GALLEGO
(*GALICIAN RICE PUDDING*)

SERVINGS: 4

Prepare Rice Pudding as directed in the preceding recipe. When rice is cooked, put in serving dish, let cool for 5 minutes, then sprinkle with a good coating of sugar and put under hot broiler until the sugar carmelizes. In Galicia, this pudding is eaten hot, but it is also good cold.

ARROZ CON LECHE CON CHANTILLY
(*RICE PUDDING WITH WHIPPED CREAM*)

The following recipe for rich, creamy Basque rice pudding is from the restaurant Aranzabi in Amasa, between San Sebastián and Tolosa. The quality of the cream and milk from the handsome brown cows kept by this farmhouse converted into a restaurant makes this a superb dessert.

SERVINGS: 4

4⅓ cups milk
½ cup plus 2 TB *rice*
1½ cups sugar
2 cinnamon sticks

½ cup whipping cream
1 tsp sugar
a little powdered cinnamon

Heat milk with cinnamon sticks. When milk has boiled, remove cinnamon and add rice. Let it cook slowly approximately 25 minutes or until rice is done. Add sugar. Let it cook another 5 minutes. Stir to prevent its sticking to pan. Put in a serving dish and chill.

Whip the cream; add a teaspoon of sugar when cream thickens. Serve pudding topped with whipped cream sprinkled with a little powdered cinnamon.

TORTA DE ARROZ CON LECHE
(*RICE PUDDING CAKE*)

SERVINGS: 8

1 cup rice
¾ cup sugar
4½ cups milk
3 eggs, separated
1 vanilla bean

a bit of lemon peel
a good pinch of salt
currant or gooseberry jelly or apricot jam for sauce

Scald rice as follows: Boil in several cups water for 3 minutes while stirring. Strain and rinse under cold running water.

Heat 2½ cups milk with lemon peel and vanilla bean broken in two. When milk boils, pour in rice slowly. Add sugar and salt. Cook on low boil for 50–60 minutes or until rice is well cooked. Add remaining milk, boiling hot, in small quantities from time to time during cooking. Remove vanilla bean and lemon peel and let rice cool.

Preheat oven to 400°. When rice is cool, stir in egg yolks; fold in egg whites beaten stiff. Put mixture in buttered mold powdered with sugar and bake in 400° oven in pan of water for 50 minutes or until done. Cake has finished baking when it is browned and springs back into place if touched with a finger. Serve cold, unmolded, with sauce of melted, hot currant or gooseberry jelly, or hot apricot jam strained through a sieve.

NOTE: Keeps well for several days in refrigerator.

LECHE FRITA
(FRIED CUSTARD SQUARES)
SERVINGS: 5–6 (34 squares)

3 cups milk	½ cup dry bread
½ cup cornstarch	crumbs
6 TB sugar	2 TB butter
1 beaten egg	2 TB olive oil
cinnamon and sugar for dusting	

Mix cornstarch, milk, and sugar in pan. Cook over low heat while stirring until very thick (10–15 minutes). Pour into cooled flat dish placed over cold water. Allow to solidify in a cool place or in refrigerator for 2 hours.

Cut into 1½-inch squares with knife dipped in cold water. Dip squares in beaten egg, then in bread crumbs. Fry in 2 TB butter mixed with 2 TB olive oil and heated until it bubbles. Brown squares on both sides, dust them in sugar mixed with a little cinnamon, and serve hot.

PAN DE SANTA TERESA

Pan de Santa Teresa is a Catalan version of what we know as French toast. There are local variations under diverse names all over Spain; this is one of the best.

SERVINGS: 4–6 (12 slices)

12 *slices of white bread (approximately ⅜" thick)*

2 *cups milk*

2 TB *sugar*

1 *cinnamon stick*

a piece of lemon peel

3 *eggs*

mixture of cinnamon and sugar for sprinkling toast

½ *cup olive oil for frying*

a pinch of salt

Boil milk for a few minutes with sugar, cinnamon stick, and lemon peel until liquid has taken on flavor. Strain liquid over bread in shallow platter.

Beat eggs in a deep plate with a pinch of salt. Remove bread slices from milk with great care, dip in egg, and fry on both sides in hot oil until browned and crusty. Serve hot, sprinkled with cinnamon and sugar mixture.

CREMA DE LA DAMA BLANCA
(*VANILLA ICE CREAM*)

The Spanish title, translated literally, is "White Lady Ice Cream." Served with chocolate sauce, it becomes "White Lady in Devil's Robes," and with strawberry sauce, "White Lady in Purple."

SERVINGS: 14

4⅓ *cups whipping cream*

3⅓ *cups milk*

1 *cup water*

¾ *cup very fine granulated sugar*

1 *vanilla bean or* 1 *tsp vanilla extract*

Boil sugar and water in uncovered pot for 15 minutes or until it forms a syrup which will fall in a ribbon from a spoon dipped in the mixture and held vertically above it. Flavor milk with vanilla extract or boil it slowly for 5 minutes with vanilla bean broken in two. Add milk to cooled syrup and mix thoroughly. Put mixture in ice trays in freezing compartment for several hours.

When milk is lightly frozen, remove from ice trays and fold in stiffly beaten whipping cream. Return to ice trays and put back in freezing compartment.

When cream is solid, remove it from trays and beat it until foamy with electric mixer or wire whisk. Return to freezing compartment in ice trays or a cake or pudding mold. Leave in freezer until it is the consistency of ice cream (about 4 hours), but do not allow it to become brick-hard; lower temperature of freezing compartment if necessary.

Just before serving, unmold on a chilled platter or form balls with an ice cream scoop and pile them in a chilled bowl (this ice cream melts rapidly). Serve with a chocolate sauce or strawberry sauce made by steeping whole wild and domestic strawberries in hot raspberry jelly until jelly cools to lukewarm.

BRAZO DE GITANO
(ROLLED CAKE WITH CREAM FILLING)

SERVINGS: 6–8

5 eggs, separated
2/3 cup sugar
1 cup cake flour

1 TB water
1/4 tsp salt
confectioners' sugar for dusting

Preheat oven to 425°. Beat egg yolks, sugar, salt, and water until creamy and thick. Add flour and beat just enough to blend. Fold in stiffly beaten egg whites. Spread evenly in 11-by-16-inch baking pan lined with wax paper. (If you have no large shallow pan, spread cake out on heavy white paper on cookie sheet. It will hold the shape you give it.) Bake 10–15 minutes or until it is lightly browned on top and springs back when touched with a finger. Turn it upside down on a sheet of wax paper sprinkled with powdered sugar. Allow to cool before removing baking paper.

When cake is cool, trim ragged edges, spread with filling, and roll up with the aid of the wax paper on the bottom. The cake should be made several hours in advance and kept in a cool place or a refrigerator. Dust with confectioners' sugar just before serving.

NOTE: Brazo de Gitano can be made with a number of fillings; two recipes for fillings follow.

CREMA PASTELERA AL RON
(RUM CUSTARD FILLING)

SERVINGS: enough for 1 Brazo de Gitano (p. 206) or a Layer Spongecake (p. 209)

2¾ cups milk	¼ cup dark rum
½ cup sugar	1 vanilla bean cut in
3 egg yolks	pieces
3 TB cornstarch	2 TB butter

Put milk, vanilla bean, and rum to cook. Boil slowly at least 5 minutes. Beat sugar, cornstarch, and egg yolks until creamy and thick. Let milk cool about 5 minutes before straining into egg mixture. Beat constantly as you add.

Cook, stirring frequently, over low flame until it thickens (approximately 20 minutes). Do not let it boil. Just before removing from fire, add butter and stir until melted and blended.

CREMA QUEMADA
(CARAMELIZED CUSTARD FILLING)
SERVINGS: enough for 1 Brazo de Gitano (p. 206) or a Layer Spongecake (p. 209)

3 cups milk	2 sticks cinnamon
1 cup sugar	peel of 1 lemon
4 egg yolks	1½ TB butter
3 TB cornstarch	

Bring milk to a boil with lemon peel and cinnamon broken in small pieces. Let it boil slowly at least 5 minutes to take on flavor. Beat egg yolks with ½ cup sugar and 3 TB cornstarch until light in color and stiff. Allow milk to cool for 5 minutes. Strain it into egg yolk mixture, blend, and stir frequently while cooking over low heat for 20 minutes or until mixture thickens. Do not allow to boil. Just before removing from fire, add 1½ TB butter and stir until melted and blended.

Let mixture cool to lukewarm before spreading on spongecake. Sprinkle remaining sugar on top of filling and put under hot broiler just long enough to caramelize sugar slightly. When sugar bubbles and begins to turn brown, it is done.

NOTE: The custard filling can be given any flavor you choose. For example, instead of cinnamon, you might use a vanilla bean, a teaspoon of almond extract, or a piece of orange peel.

BIZCOCHO CON CREMA
(SPONGECAKE WITH CREAM FILLING)

SERVINGS: a two-layer cake, 11" x 9"

7 eggs, separated	1 TB dark rum
1 cup sugar	½ tsp salt
1⅓ cups flour	1 recipe Rum Custard
1 TB lemon juice	Filling (p. 207)
grated rind of 1 lemon	¼ cup powdered sugar

Preheat oven to 425°. Beat yolks with grated lemon rind until light yellow. Add sugar and salt. Beat until stiff. Add lemon juice and rum; mix. Add flour and beat just enough to mix. Beat egg whites to stiff peak, adding 3 drops of lemon juice as eggs begin to whiten. Fold into cake dough and spread dough evenly in two pans lined with wax paper (or buttered and sprinkled with flour). Bake 15 minutes or until cake is lightly browned and springs back when pressed with finger. Turn each layer upside down on paper sprinkled with powdered sugar and let cool before removing the paper on which the cake baked. (If you do not use paper to line cake pans, invert pans and do not try to remove layers until they cool.)

Spread rum custard filling thickly between the two layers. Sprinkle top of cake with powdered sugar just before serving.

BIZCOCHO DE ALMENDRAS
(ALMOND SPONGECAKE)

SERVINGS: a 9" loaf cake

1 cup blanched almonds	1⅛ cups cake flour
	a pinch of salt
6 eggs	¼ cup powdered sugar
1 cup sugar	

Preheat oven to 375°. Grind almonds in electric blender or pound in mortar to fine paste. Beat three whole eggs and three yolks with sugar and salt until thick and light yellow. Fold in three egg whites beaten to stiff peak. Gradually sift in flour mixed with ground almonds. Fold no more than necessary to make an evenly blended mixture. Pour into 9-inch loaf pan either lined with wax paper or lightly buttered and sprinkled with flour. Bake 25–30 minutes in 375° oven or until toothpick inserted in middle of cake comes out clean.

Invert cake over rack or wax paper sprinkled with powdered sugar. If you have used wax paper, cake will come out instantly; wait until it cools to remove the paper on which it baked. If you have not used paper, leave cake inverted in pan until cool. Sprinkle with powdered sugar just before serving.

TARTA DE ALMENDRAS
(ALMOND CAKE)
SERVINGS: a one-layer cake, 8″ x 12″

1 cup blanched almonds	2 TB dark rum
2/3 cup sugar	a pinch of salt
1/2 cup cake flour	powdered sugar for dusting cake
3 whole eggs	

Preheat oven to 350°. Beat eggs with sugar until creamy and thick. Grind almonds to fine powder in electric blender or pound in mortar. Mix ground almonds with flour and salt and add to eggs with rum. Stir just enough to blend. Pour into 8-by-12-inch baking pan lined with waxed paper (or buttered and sprinkled with flour). Bake in 350° oven 25–30 minutes or until cake pulls away from sides of pan and springs back when pressed lightly with finger. Turn upside down on cake rack or wax paper sprinkled with powdered sugar. Remove paper from bottom of cake when cool. (If you do not use paper for baking, leave cake inverted in pan until cool.)

Sprinkle with powdered sugar just before serving.

TARTA DE SANTIAGO
(*GALICIAN ALMOND CAKE* [*from Santiago de Compostela*])

SERVINGS: a high, round one-layer cake, 9″ in diameter

2 *cups blanched almonds*	6 *eggs*
3 TB *butter*	*grated rind of 1 lemon*
⅔ *cup sugar*	¼ *tsp powdered cinnamon*

¼ *cup sugar for topping*

Preheat oven to 425°. Mix butter with sugar and cinnamon. Separately, beat eggs with grated lemon rind until foamy. Grind almonds to fine paste in electric blender or mortar. Add all but ¼ cup almonds and beaten eggs to butter and sugar mixture (reserve remaining almonds for topping). Mix only enough to blend well. Pour into 9-inch round cake pan which has been lightly buttered and sprinkled with flour. Bake 25–30 minutes in 425° oven. Cake is done when a toothpick inserted in the middle comes out clean and cake springs back if pressed with a finger. Invert cake until it cools before removing.

Place cooled cake on cookie sheet, coat top of cake with the remaining ground almonds and ½ cup sugar, and place under broiler until topping forms a light crust. Do not allow sugar to caramelize: it should merely brown and harden slightly. The cake should be coarse-grained and of a rich yellow color.

FRIED BANANA PASTRIES

SERVINGS: 30–35 pastries 3″ long

4–5 *bananas*
1 recipe for Empana-
dillas Valencianas
(p. 110)
⅓ *cup olive oil for fry-*
ing

powdered sugar for
dusting (substitute
granulated sugar if
you prefer)

Chill dough several hours in refrigerator before rolling. Roll dough rather thin (⅛ inch) on lightly floured surface. Cut bananas lengthwise in slices approximately ¼ inch thick. Halve slices and roll each one in the dough. Press down edge to seal and tamp ends to close. Fry in hot olive oil until browned on all sides. Dust liberally with powdered sugar and serve. The pastry is flaky and the banana melts into a creamy filling.

BUÑUELOS DE LIMON
(*LEMON CRULLERS*)

SERVINGS: 18 crullers

1 egg
grated rind of 1 lemon
4 TB *sugar*
1 TB *water*
a pinch of salt

2 TB *olive oil for batter*
¾ *cup olive oil for fry-*
ing
2 *tsp lemon juice*
1¼ *cups flour*

1 tsp baking powder

Beat egg, grated lemon rind, sugar, water, and salt in bowl. When mixture is light and foamy, add 2 TB olive oil and lemon juice. Mix in flour and baking powder.

Heat oil until it begins to crinkle. Drop dough off tip of

tablespoon into hot oil; take care to drop dough in one rounded lump. The crullers should puff and brown almost instantly. Turn them, brown the second side, remove, drain on paper, and immediately roll in granulated sugar. If the edges are ragged or the dough spatters on being dropped into the oil, the oil is too hot.

Good lukewarm or cold, they are best the day they are made.

PESTIÑOS ANDALUCES
(ANDALUSIAN CRULLERS)

SERVINGS: 3 dozen crullers

grated rind of 1 lemon
juice of 1 medium lemon
4 TB milk
6 TB olive oil
⅛ tsp cinnamon
¼ tsp salt
4 TB anise liqueur (substitute any dry liqueur if anise is not available)

4 cups flour (approximate)
½–¾ cup olive oil for frying
¾ cup sugar for syrup
½ cup water
¼ cup anise liqueur (or another dry liqueur) for syrup

Put grated rind, lemon juice, milk, cinnamon, salt, 4 TB anise liqueur, and 6 TB olive oil in a bowl. Mix well. Stir in flour until dough is stiff (approximately 4 cups flour). Let dough rest 1 hour in a cool place.

Divide dough into four parts, roll it out very thin on a lightly floured surface, and cut it into rectangles about 3 by 2 inches. Heat frying oil to the verge of smoking. Roll up the rectangles and fry them, a few at a time, in the hot oil. Drain on a rack or brown paper.

Make a syrup by melting ¾ cup sugar with ½ cup

water. When it bubbles and starts to thicken, add ¼ cup anise liqueur. Dip the fried crullers in the hot liquid and drain them on a rack. Sprinkle with sugar while still warm. Let them cool before serving.

POLVORONES SEVILLANOS
(SEVILLIAN CINNAMON COOKIES)

SERVINGS: 3 dozen small cookies

3½ cups sifted flour
⅔ cup lard
½ cup sugar
1 egg yolk

⅓ cup of any dry liqueur
2 tsp powdered cinnamon
a pinch of salt

powdered sugar for sprinkling

Preheat oven to 325°. Dissolve sugar in liqueur mixed with egg yolk. Cream lard with cinnamon. Add sugar-egg yolk mixture. Sift flour with salt onto table or marble slab. Make a hollow in center of flour and pour in the other ingredients. Blend well with hands. The dough should be very stiff like the French *pâte sablée*. If too crumbly to handle, blend in a little water. Roll out ⅓ inch thick on floured surface. Cut with cookie cutter (oval is traditional). Bake on floured cookie sheets in 325° oven for 20 minutes or until firm to touch. The cookies will be done when they barely begin to turn brown (they should not be allowed to brown). Before serving, sprinkle heavily with powdered sugar.

ALMENDRADOS (I)
(ALMOND COOKIES)

SERVINGS: 2 dozen cookies, 2½–3″ in diameter

1 cup toasted almonds   3 large egg whites
⅔ cup sugar

Preheat oven to 350°. Grind almonds to a fine paste in electric blender or mortar. Mix with sugar and add egg whites beaten just enough to blend. The mixture should be thick enough to hold the shape of a cookie when dropped from a spoon.

Drop heaping teaspoonfuls onto buttered cookie tins and bake until browned (12–15 minutes). Cookies will be soft when removed, but will become crisp as they cool on rack.

ALMENDRADOS (II)
(ALMOND COOKIES)

SERVINGS: 20 cookies

1⅓ cups blanched al-
monds

10 blanched almonds
split in two length-
wise for garnishing
cookies

⅔ cup sugar

2 egg whites

a pinch of salt

Preheat oven to 400°. Grind the 1⅓ cups blanched almonds to a fine paste in electric blender or mortar. Mix ground almonds with sugar and salt. Fold in egg whites beaten to a stiff peak. For each cookie, drop equivalent of heaping ½ tsp of mixture onto buttered sheet. Top each cookie with half an almond. Bake in 400° oven until cookies are lightly browned on top (approximately 10 minutes). The inside of the cookie will look still moist when the cookie is done. Remove to a rack and cool.

PANELLETS
(CATALAN ALMOND COOKIES)

Panellets are rich almond cookies made in every peasant household in Catalonia for the eve of All Saints Day

215

and eaten accompanied by roasted chestnuts and aged wine. *Panellets* are best a day or two after baking. They keep very well and are always made in quantities. The recipe given below makes enough to fill the cookie jar, but is only half what any peasant household would undertake at a time.

1 lb. blanched almonds
1 lb. sugar
2 medium potatoes
1 egg
pine nuts, slivered almonds, toasted hazelnuts, candied fruit, and sugar for garnishing cookies (all in small quantities)

1 package vanilla pudding mix
1 tsp vanilla extract
grated rind of ½ lemon
1 TB cognac or rum

Preheat oven to 500°. Grind almonds to a fine paste in mortar or electric blender (½ cup at a time). Boil potatoes and mash them. Mix all ingredients except garnish in a large bowl. Work paste with hands until well blended. With wet hands, form cakes the diameter of a silver dollar, but high and rounded. Put a toasted hazelnut on some; on others, a piece of candied fruit. Dip some in pine nuts, sugar, or slivered almonds. Dip bottom of cookie in flour and put on greased tray in 500° oven for a few minutes. Watch closely and remove cookies as soon as they are lightly browned. When hot, cookies will taste not quite done, but they will be just right when cooled.

NOTE: If you start with almonds in the shell as the peasants do, shell and scald them the day before you bake (see p. 40). Spread them out to dry. If they are not completely dry when you want to use them, put them in a slow oven for 10 minutes.

PICATOSTES
(FRIED SUGARED BREAD)

Picatostes are served with hot chocolate for the late afternoon snack known as the *merienda*. They must be freshly made.

½ loaf of day-old, un-
sliced white bread
1 cup milk
1 cup water
¼–½ cup powdered sugar

⅓ cup flour
½ cup olive oil for fry-
ing
a pinch of salt

Cut bread in slices ¾ inch thick. Cut slices lengthwise and crosswise to form cubes. Mix milk, water, and salt in bowl. Soak cubes, drain, and place on cloth or kitchen towel. Keep covered until you are ready to use them.

Just before serving, dip cubes in flour and fry until golden in very hot olive oil. Sprinkle with powdered sugar and serve piled in a pyramid on a platter.

BIZCOCHOS BORRACHOS DE GUADALAJARA
(TIPSY TEA CAKES)

SERVINGS: approximately 3 dozen 2½″ squares

6 eggs, separated
⅔ cup sugar for cake
dough
1¾ cups flour
2 cups sweet white wine

⅔ cup sugar for syrup
sugar and a little cinna-
mon for dusting
cakes

Preheat oven to 375°. Beat yolks with ⅔ cup sugar. When creamy yellow, add flour. Beat just enough to blend. Fold in six egg whites beaten to stiff peak. Pour dough into paper-lined pan approximately 9 by 11 inches. Bake in 375° oven until cake springs back when touched with finger and is golden brown on top (about 30 minutes). Allow to cool on cake rack before removing paper.

Melt ⅔ cup sugar in saucepan until sugar caramelizes, then add 2 cups sweet wine. Cut cooled cake into squares. Heat and stir syrup until it is well mixed. Dip squares in syrup, roll them in a mixture of sugar and a little cinnamon and let them dry in a well-aired place.

CHAPTER 15

PATIO DISHES

SPANISH peasants do not take sandwiches on picnics or to the fields: they cook their food on the spot. Their customs are particularly well suited to patio or backyard cooking.

You need no elaborate barbecue—within minutes, the peasants build a good cooking fire or make a spread of coals for broiling anywhere. For the former, simply place three stones in a triangle close enough to support a wide, low cooking dish. Build a fire of dry twigs in the middle and keep adding to the twigs as long as you need a hot fire; spread them out if necessary to reduce the flame. If you use larger wood, keep all the logs pointing toward the center and burning only at the center; as the logs burn, push them in toward each other. For broiling, replace the cooking dish with an improvised grill of chicken wire (or use an old oven rack from the kitchen stove).

219

Many recipes in the preceding sections are as good if not better cooked in the open. Among the dishes most suitable for outdoor cooking are the simpler omelets (Chapter Six), all the paellas and rices (Chapter Seven), Mussels in Tomato Sauce (p. 117), Clams in White Wine (p. 118), Grilled Lamb Chops with All-i-oli (p. 168) or Romesco Sauce (p. 168), and Grilled Sausage. Empanada Gallega can be taken on picnics cooked and ready to eat. The recipes included in this chapter are those which almost *must* be made and eaten outdoors.

GARLIC BREAD

Those who like garlic will find this delicious. Toast thick slices of bread over a fire on long sticks or forks, rub hot toast with peeled garlic cloves, pour olive oil over it, sprinkle lightly with salt, and eat, preferably accompanied by a dry white wine.

TOMATO BREAD

Olive oil and tomato replace butter for sandwiches in the olive-growing parts of Spain. The pulp of a ripe tomato is rubbed on a piece of bread or toast, often previously rubbed with garlic. It is sprinkled liberally with olive oil, lightly with salt, and is then eaten with a grilled pork sausage, a slice of cured ham, a cold omelet, or anything else you choose.

GRILLED ARTICHOKES

Peel tough outer leaves of medium-size artichokes. Cut off tops and spread leaves until choke is like a half-opened flower. Rub chokes with olive oil and salt and put them face down on a grill over hot coals for 7–8 minutes. Turn right side up, pour olive oil and a little vinegar down between the leaves, sprinkle with salt, and cook until tender (another 5 minutes or so). Very messy but very good.

ROASTED ONION

Bury a sweet onion in its skin in hot coals. When it has cooked approximately 1 hour and is tender when pricked, peel it and eat with olive oil and a little salt.

ESCALIVADA
(ROASTED PEPPER, EGGPLANT, AND TOMATO)

While the *escalivada* can be made indoors, its flavor is incomparably improved when the vegetables are cooked over a wood or charcoal fire. Throw green and red peppers and eggplants on hot coals or directly in fire. Roast tomatoes briefly on grill or over dying embers. Turn peppers and eggplants from time to time until all skin is blackened (but not calcinated). Strip off peel with fingers while vegetables are still hot. Cut peeled vegetables into long strips; arrange decoratively in a platter with whole grilled tomatoes. Sprinkle olive oil liberally over all and salt lightly.

Escalivada is delicious as a hot vegetable with grilled meats and chops, as an hors d'oeuvre, or as a cold salad. On picnics, the grilled peppers and eggplants are often spread on tomato bread (p. 220) and eaten with grilled sausage on top. To make it indoors, bake peppers and eggplant in a moderately hot oven 45 minutes before peeling. An alternate method is to coat the peppers and eggplant with oil, fry on all sides, and cook slowly, covered, on top of stove for about 30 minutes or until peel comes off easily. The tomatoes can be roasted, grilled, or fried whole.

221

THE CALÇOTADA

This is the specialty of Valls in the province of Tarragona. Now there are grills for making the *calçotada* in farmhouses and inns around the town for the benefit of excursionists from Barcelona and tourists, but the *calçotada* used to be the prelude to a family feast in the fields which coincided with the arrival of warmer weather and the maturing of the *calçot*.

In December and January, the shoot that sprouts from the onions stored for winter is removed from the onion along with the bulb it has formed in the center of the vegetable. The shoot is planted, watered once and no more, and grows by itself into a *calçot*, which looks like an oversized and bulbous spring onion. A large spring onion is, in fact, the best substitute for it. To be suitable, it must be large enough so that something is left when the charred outer surface is peeled off.

The cooking of the *calçot* is very simple: it is grilled until well blackened over fairly hot coals. Eating it is more difficult, and the inns of Valls provide paper bibs for their clients and arrange for handwashing and a complete change of table after the consumption of the *calçots*. The best way to separate the sweet, tender white part from the charred surface is to pinch the bulb at the bottom while pulling on the green sprout. The unblackened part will pop out, ready to be dipped in a sauce and eaten.

A variety of sauces is served: one of the best is Salsa Colorada (p. 192). The *calçotada* is traditionally followed by lamb chops grilled over the same fire and served with All-i-oli (p. 168).

GRILLED SMALL FISH

If you are fortunate enough to be able to get fresh sardines or fresh anchovy, grill them over hot glowing coals or wood embers. Dust fish lightly in flour before grilling: the flour will help to keep the fish whole. If using larger fish, such as mackerel, score the sides lightly in two or three places. Put fish on a hot grill, turn when browned, and remove when well browned on both sides. Sprinkle a few drops of olive oil over fish while grilling. When it is cooked, sprinkle it with finely chopped garlic and parsley, and pour hot olive oil over it. The hot oil will cook the garlic and parsley slightly and permeate the flesh of the fish with the flavoring.

BESUGO A LA DONOSTIARRA
(*CHARCOAL GRILLED SEA BREAM*)

After being cleaned, the fish should be salted and left with salt for an hour (or more). To grill, put the fish on a hot gridiron over glowing coals or wood embers. Brush fish with oil from time to time and turn frequently until the skin is well toasted and the fish cooked through. Just before serving, fry two cloves of garlic in olive oil (⅓–½ cup olive oil for 4–5 pounds of fish). Discard garlic when browned. Add the juice of 1 lemon and reheat. Open fish and pour hot mixture over it.

GRILLED PEPPERY FISH

Grill any white fish as in the preceding recipe. Just before serving, fry four or five cloves of garlic in olive oil with two or more pieces of hot chili pepper. (If hot peppers are not available, substitute powdered cayenne, adding it only when the garlic cloves are browned.) Open the fish and strain the hot oil over it.

GRILLED RABBIT

SERVINGS: 6

2 *dressed, cleaned*   *double recipe All-i-oli*
whole rabbits   *with Mustard (p.*
½ *glass white wine*   *190)*

Rinse inside of rabbit with white wine. Brush rabbit liberally with all-i-oli sauce. In Catalonia, the rabbit is sometimes speared in spreadeagle position on sticks and braced on stones over a campfire of rosemary bush, but it can also be put on a hot grill over glowing coals or wood embers. Turn at least twice during cooking and baste with all-i-oli often enough to keep rabbit moist. Serve with remaining sauce in which pieces of rabbit are dipped as they are eaten.

APPENDIX AND INDEX

COOKING HINTS

ALMONDS.   To scald, put almonds in boiling water off the fire for 30 seconds or until the almond slips out of its skin easily when squeezed between the fingers. Strain almonds, rinse under cold water, and peel at once. To keep scalded almonds, spread out in well-ventilated spot to allow moisture to evaporate, then put in slow oven for 10 minutes and allow to cool before storing. For toasting of almonds, see page 40.

BREAD.   Served with meat in sauce, bread fried in olive oil makes a delicious substitute for potatoes.

BUTTER.   When frying with butter, add a little olive oil to the butter to keep it from scorching.

COD.   To desalt dried cod, soak overnight in several changes of cool water.

EGGS.   To add egg yolks to a sauce, stir a little cool or lukewarm liquid into the yolks before gradually blending hot sauce into them.

To poach eggs, break each individually on a saucer and slide it into the liquid. Eggs poached apart from a sauce are put in boiling salt water with 1 TB vinegar for 4 minutes, then scooped out with a slotted spoon and put in cold water. The ragged edges may be trimmed with kitchen scissors.

FISH.   To boil, cover with cold water, bring slowly to a boil, and simmer until fish is cooked through. Fish slices are done when center bone begins to be detached from flesh of fish. To broil, coat fish lightly with flour and put on hot grid. If broiling large fish, score sides lightly with knife in two or three places to allow heat to penetrate evenly.

227

LEFTOVERS

All-i-oli. Use on cold vegetable salads, on hot boiled vegetables (such as green beans and potatoes), on cold meat canapés, with cold vegetable salad in cocktail tartlets (p. 49) and in Gambas al Ajillo (p. 120).

Asparagus tips. Use in omelets (p. 86), Huevos al Plato a la Flamenca (p. 90), or any of a number of fish dishes: Merluza a lo Jaizkibel (p. 132), Merluza Koskera (p. 134), Merluza en Salsa Verde (p. 136), Merluza a lo Vasco (p. 137).

Chicken. Use in Buñuelitos (p. 47), in Canapé of Puréed Chicken (p. 42), or with mayonnaise in cocktail tartlets (p. 49).

Fish stock. Leftover fish stock is preferable to water for poaching fish. It can be substituted for water in any fish dish calling for a few tablespoons of water. It is recommended in Arroz Abanda (p. 102) and called for in Sopa de Ajo al Pescado (p. 72).

Green beans. Use in Tortilla a la Paisana (p. 88) and Huevos al Plato a la Flamenca (p. 90).

Ham. Use in Buñuelitos (p. 47), in Empanadillas Valencianas (p. 110), Tortilla de Patata a la Española (p. 85) or Tortilla a la Paisana (p. 88), or fry with spinach (p. 178).

Lamb. Leftover lamb is very good in Cordero Cochifrito (p. 167).

Meat. Bits of meat can always be put in omelets with leftover cooked vegetables or potatoes or can be used in empanadillas (pp. 48–49) and empanadas (p. 109).

Pastry dough. Leftover unsweetened dough can be used for cocktail tartlets (p. 49), for empanadillas (pp. 48–49) and empanadas (p. 109), and for Fried Banana Pastries (p. 212).

Peas. Use in Tortilla a la Paisana (p. 88), Huevos al Plato a la Flamenca (p. 90), Merluza a lo Jaizkibel (p. 132), Merluza Koskera (p. 134), and Merluza en Salsa Verde (p. 136).

Potatoes. Leftover boiled potatoes can be used in Tortilla a la Paisana (p. 88).

Romesco. Leftover Romesco Sauce can be used on hot boiled vegetables and on cold meat canapés.

MOLLUSKS. Once cleaned, mollusks such as clams and mussels should be left to soak in clear, cold water for at least an hour to disgorge sand. When clams or mussels have been opened apart and the juice is to be used in a dish, strain juice through a kitchen towel or pour it off carefully to ensure leaving behind any remaining particles of sand.

OLIVE OIL. In cooking with olive oil, the temperature of the oil is of paramount importance. For frying almost all foods except a few delicate fritters, oil should be heated to the verge of smoking before the food is put in. This ensures a crisp outside and prevents overabsorption of oil. For blending with fish juices or flour, or for frying garlic or onion in small quantities without browning them, the oil should be barely simmering. For adding to raw garlic or egg yolks to make sauces, it should be at room temperature.

Olive oil can be used again and again for frying. It is little trouble to keep two jars for used olive oil in the kitchen with a small strainer on top; leftover oil is simply poured through the strainer from the frying pan and is ready for reuse. (Two jars are necessary in order to keep oil in which fish has been fried separate.)

ONIONS. It is worth the trouble to chop onions very fine when chopped or minced onions are called for.

Minced onions blend into the sauce and give it both richer flavor and smoother consistency.

PAPRIKA. Because it burns easily, paprika is usually stirred in over low heat or with the pan off the fire. Once liquid is added to a sauce containing paprika, the danger of burning it is past.

PEPPERS. The easiest way to prepare peppers for peeling is to put them directly on hot coals or in a fire until charred. For methods using the kitchen stove, see Escalivada (p. 221).

The dried peppers called for in certain recipes are ripe red peppers which have been threaded on a string and hung up in the fall to dry in a well-ventilated place. Before use, dried peppers are soaked overnight in water. If dried peppers are not obtainable, substitute fresh peppers or canned pimiento and add a little paprika to the dish.

SAFFRON. Saffron is usually crushed in a mortar or bowl and diluted with a little liquid before being added to a sauce. To reduce its acridity, fold it in a piece of paper and place it in the oven or on a hot surface to toast. The saffron is toasted as soon as the paper begins to turn brown.

SALAD GREENS. The careful drying of salad greens is an important element in the flavor of the dressing. To avoid having to dry each leaf separately in a towel, wash the salad long in advance, shake it thoroughly in a wire salad basket, hang it up to let the water evaporate during 1–2 hours, then roll it in a kitchen towel and store it in the refrigerator. Salad prepared this way will keep well for 24 hours or more.

SAUCES. Pounded almonds or mashed fried bread may be used instead of flour or cornstarch to thicken a sauce. If a sauce is too thin when a dish is completed, remove sauce, boil it down, and return it to dish. To make a sauce smooth, strain it.

TOMATOES. Always use ripe tomatoes in sauces; green tomatoes give a sour taste. If necessary, add a pinch of sugar to compensate for acidity of tomatoes.

The peel of tomatoes is unattractive in sauces. Unless the sauce is to be strained, peel tomato after dipping briefly in very hot or boiling water to loosen skin. Sometimes the tomato is also seeded (gently squeezed to remove seeds).

VINEGAR. When using vinegar in a sauce, let it boil down to cook out acidity.

WINE. The alcohol must be evaporated from wine and liquor used in cooking. This is usually done by boiling until liquid reduces to half. The flaming of cognac is another way of evaporating alcohol.

TABLE OF EQUIVALENT MEASUREMENTS
AND OVEN TEMPERATURES

a pinch	less than ⅛ teaspoon
3 teaspoons (tsp)	1 tablespoon (TB)
2 tablespoons	1 liquid ounce
4 tablespoons	¼ cup
16 tablespoons	1 cup
2 cups	1 pint
2 pints	1 quart
4 quarts	1 gallon
¼ pound butter	½ cup
1 pound butter	2 cups
1 pound tomatoes or 3–4 medium tomatoes	1½ cups peeled, seeded, chopped tomato
1 pound onions	3½–4 cups chopped or sliced
1 pound potatoes	3 medium potatoes
¼ pound shelled almonds	¾ cup
½ pound raw rice	1 cup raw rice or 3 cups cooked rice

OVEN TEMPERATURES

very slow	225° F.
slow	275° F.
moderate	350° F.
hot	400° F.
very hot	475° F.

GLOSSARY OF SPANISH WORDS

ajo	garlic
al, a la, a lo	in the style of; as; with
almeja	clam
almendra	almond
almuerzo	midmorning meal; first substantial meal of the day
anchoa	anchovy
arroz	rice; also cooked rice dish
asado	roast
atún	tuna
bacalao	cod
besugo	sea bream
bizcocho	spongecake
bodega	wine cellar
buñuelo	fritter
buñuelito	small fritter
butifarra	a kind of sausage (Catalan specialty)
calamar	squid
caldo	broth; stock; sauce; wine; alcohol
cena	supper
centolla	sea crab
chanquetes	small anchovy (Málagan specialty)
chorizo	sausage seasoned with ground red peppers
chuleta	chop
ciruelas	prunes
cochinillo	suckling pig
cocido	boiled; cooked; meat and vegetable soup

GLOSSARY OF SPANISH WORDS

cocina	kitchen; cuisine
col	cabbage
comida	meal; main midday meal
con	with
conejo	rabbit
cordero	lamb
crema	cream custard dessert; also cream filling for cakes
crema quemada	caramelized custard (Catalan)
croqueta	croquette
de, del, de la	of
desayuno	breakfast
empanada	turnover; pastry filled with meat, fish or vegetables
empanadilla	small empanada
emparedado	sandwich
en	in
ensalada	salad
entremés	hors d'oeuvre
entremeses variados	assorted hors d'oeuvres
escabeche	marinade
estilo	style
estofado	stew
fabada	Asturian stew of dried white beans, sausages, and meats
frito, frita	fried
gallina	hen; stewing chicken
gamba	shrimp
gazpacho	Andalusian specialty, usually liquid and made primarily with vegetables
guisantes	peas
huevo	egg
huevo duro	hard-boiled egg
huevos al plato	baked eggs

jamón	ham
judía	bean
lacón	cured foreham (Galician specialty)
langosta	lobster
leche	milk
lenguado	sole
limón	lemon
lomo de cerdo	loin of pork
mahonesa	mayonnaise
mejillones	mussels
merienda	late-afternoon snack or meal
merluza	hake
mero	halibut
naranja	orange
olla	jar; pot; term for meat and vegetable soup in Basque provinces, Catalonia, and Córdoba
paella	Valencian-style pan for cooking rice; a classic rice dish
pan	bread
pasas	raisins
patata	potato
pelota	meat dumpling
percebes	edible rock barnacle
pescaditos	small fish
pescado	fish
picada	minced; mortar-mashed food added for seasoning or thickening sauces
pil-pil	simmered (Basque)
piñones	pine nuts; sometimes sold in North America as pignola, pignoli, or pignolia
pollito	very young chicken
pollo	chicken

pote	pot; term for meat and vegetable soup in the Asturias
puchero	pot; term for meat and vegetable soup in La Mancha
rape	frogfish (not found in N. America)
relleno	stuffed
romana, a la	dipped in flour and egg and fried
ron	rum
rovellon	a kind of mushroom (Catalan)
rustido	roast (Catalan)
salsa	sauce
shangurro	crab (Basque)
sofrito	slightly fried; term used for foundation of many Spanish sauces, usually made of tomato and onion fried slowly in olive oil
sopa	soup
tallarines	noodles
tallina	a kind of small clam
tapa	appetizer; lid
tarta	cake; tart
tartaleta	tartlet
té quemada	Basque after-dinner drink
ternera	veal
tomate	tomato
torta	round cake; pie
tortilla	omelet
trucha	trout
turrón	sweet dessert
unto	aged, smoked bacon (Galician specialty)
vieira	sea scallop
vinagreta	vinegar sauce (Catalan)
y	and

INDEX

244

BARBARA NORMAN

———————◆———————

Born in a Chicago suburb, Barbara Norman
earned her B.A. at Stanford University and sub-
sequently worked and lived in Washington,
D.C., Munich and Paris. She resigned from the
U.S. Embassy in Paris in 1957 following her
marriage to concert violinist Paul Makano-
witzky. Since then she has translated several
Russian classics into English for publication under her married name while moving from New
York to Paris and back to New York. She and
her husband now live in Setauket, Long Island,
but plan to return whenever possible to their
house in Spain.